BASS GUITAR
SCALES
ENCYCLOPEDIA

Fast Reference for the Scales You Need in Every Key

ANDY SCHNEIDER

SEEING MUSIC
METHOD BOOKS

CONTENTS

SPELLING SCALES — 7

MAJOR TYPES — 7
MINOR TYPES — 8
DOMINANT TYPES — 10
AUGMENTED TYPES — 11
DIMINISHED TYPES — 11
CHROMATIC TYPE — 12

SCALES WITH ROOT = A — 13

MAJOR TYPES — 13
MINOR TYPES — 16
DOMINANT TYPES — 23
AUGMENTED TYPES — 24
DIMINISHED TYPES — 25

SCALES WITH ROOT = A SHARP/B FLAT — 27

MAJOR TYPES — 27
MINOR TYPES — 30
DOMINANT TYPES — 37
AUGMENTED TYPES — 38
DIMINISHED TYPES — 39

SEEING MUSIC
METHOD BOOKS

SCALES WITH ROOT = B   41

MAJOR TYPES   *41*
MINOR TYPES   *44*
DOMINANT TYPES   *51*
AUGMENTED TYPES   *52*
DIMINISHED TYPES   *53*

SCALES WITH ROOT = C   55

MAJOR TYPES   *55*
MINOR TYPES   *58*
DOMINANT TYPES   *65*
AUGMENTED TYPES   *66*
DIMINISHED TYPES   *67*

SCALES WITH ROOT = C SHARP/D FLAT   69

MAJOR TYPES   *69*
MINOR TYPES   *72*
DOMINANT TYPES   *79*
AUGMENTED TYPES   *80*
DIMINISHED TYPES   *81*

SCALES WITH ROOT = D   83

MAJOR TYPES   *83*
MINOR TYPES   *86*
DOMINANT TYPES   *93*
AUGMENTED TYPES   *94*
DIMINISHED TYPES   *95*

SCALES WITH ROOT = D SHARP/E FLAT   97

MAJOR TYPES   *97*
MINOR TYPES   *100*
DOMINANT TYPES   *107*
AUGMENTED TYPES   *108*
DIMINISHED TYPES   *109*

SCALES WITH ROOT = E   111

MAJOR TYPES   *111*
MINOR TYPES   *114*
DOMINANT TYPES   *121*
AUGMENTED TYPES   *122*
DIMINISHED TYPES   *123*

SCALES WITH ROOT = F   125

MAJOR TYPES   *125*
MINOR TYPES   *128*
DOMINANT TYPES   *135*
AUGMENTED TYPES   *136*
DIMINISHED TYPES   *137*

SCALES WITH ROOT = F SHARP/G FLAT   139

MAJOR TYPES   *139*
MINOR TYPES   *142*
DOMINANT TYPES   *149*
AUGMENTED TYPES   *150*
DIMINISHED TYPES   *151*

SCALES WITH ROOT = G   153

MAJOR TYPES — *153*
MINOR TYPES — *156*
DOMINANT TYPES — *163*
AUGMENTED TYPES — *164*
DIMINISHED TYPES — *165*

SCALES WITH ROOT = G SHARP/A FLAT   167

MAJOR TYPES — *167*
MINOR TYPES — *170*
DOMINANT TYPES — *177*
AUGMENTED TYPES — *178*
DIMINISHED TYPES — *179*

CHROMATIC SCALES   181

BASS GUITAR SCALES ENCYCLOPEDIA

SPELLING SCALES

WHAT IS SCALE "SPELLING"?

All scales are combinations of whole and half-step intervals and on occassion larger intervals. It is the specific combination of intervals which defines a scale and makes it unique. Starting from any root, this sequence of specific intervals will define the scale. This chapter defines those step-wise combinations and provides the interval from the root to each scale tone.

MAJOR TYPES

IONIAN (MAJOR)

Intervals	R	M2	M3	P4	P5	M6	M7	R
Example	C	D	E	F	G	A	B	C

Fig.1 - Ionian Spelling

MAJOR PENTATONIC

Intervals	R	M2	M3	P5	M6	R
Example	C	D	E	G	A	C

Fig.2 - Major Pentatonic Spelling

LYDIAN

Intervals	**R**	**M2**	**M3**	**#4**	**P5**	**M6**	**M7**	**R**
Example	C	D	E	F♯	G	A	B	C

Fig.3 - Lydian Spelling

MINOR TYPES

AEOLIAN (NATURAL MINOR)

Intervals	**R**	**M2**	**m3**	**P4**	**P5**	**m6**	**m7**	**R**
Example	C	D	E♭	F	G	A♭	B♭	C

Fig.4 - Aeolian Spelling

MINOR PENTATONIC

Intervals	**R**	**m3**	**P4**	**P5**	**m7**	**R**
Example	C	E♭	F	G	B♭	C

Fig.5 - Minor Pentatonic Spelling

DORIAN

Intervals	R	M2	m3	P4	P5	M6	m7	R
Example	C	D	E♭	F	G	A	B♭	C

FIG.6 - DORIAN SPELLING

PHRYGIAN

Intervals	R	m2	m3	P4	P5	m6	m7	R
Example	C	D♭	E♭	F	G	A♭	B♭	C

FIG.7 - PHRYGIAN SPELLING

HARMONIC MINOR

Intervals	R	M2	m3	P4	P5	m6	M7	R
Example	C	D	E♭	F	G	A♭	B	C

FIG.8 - HARMONIC MINOR SPELLING

MELODIC MINOR

Ascending								
Intervals	**R**	**M2**	**m3**	**P4**	**P5**	**M6**	**M7**	**R**
Example	C	D	E♭	F	G	A	B	C

FIG.9 - MELODIC MINOR ASCENDING SPELLING

Descending								
Intervals	**R**	**m7**	**m6**	**P5**	**P4**	**m3**	**M2**	**R**
Example	C	B♭	A♭	G	F	E♭	D	C

FIG.10 - MELODIC MINOR DESCENDING SPELLING

Note: For Melodic Minor Descending, see also Aeolian.

BLUES SCALE

Intervals	**R**	**m3**	**P4**	**flat5**	**P5**	**m7**	**R**
Example	C	E♭	F	G♭	G	B♭	C

FIG.11 - BLUES SCALE SPELLING

DOMINANT TYPES

MIXOLYDIAN

Intervals	**R**	**M2**	**M3**	**P4**	**P5**	**M6**	**m7**	**R**
Example	C	D	E	F	G	A	B♭	C

FIG.12 - MIXOLYDIAN SPELLING

10 BASS GUITAR SCALES ENCYCLOPEDIA: FROM SEEING MUSIC METHOD BOOKS

AUGMENTED TYPES

WHOLE TONE

Intervals	R	M2	M3	flat5	#5	m7	R
Example	C	D	E♭	G♭	G♯	B♭	C

FIG.13 - WHOLE TONE SPELLING

DIMINISHED TYPES

LOCRIAN

Intervals	R	m2	m3	P4	flat5	m6	m7	R
Example	C	D♭	E♭	F	G♭	A♭	B♭	C

FIG.14 - LOCRIAN SPELLING

HALF/WHOLE DIMINISHED

Intervals	R	m2	m3	M3	#4	P5	M6	m7	R
Example	C	D♭	E♭	E	G♭	G	A	B♭	C

FIG.15 - HALF-WHOLE DIMINISHED SPELLING

CHROMATIC TYPE

Intervals	R	m2	M2	m3	M3	P4	flat5	P5	m6	M6	m7	M7	R
Example	C	D♭	D	E♭	E	F	G♭	G	A♭	A	B♭	B	C

Fig.16 - Chromatic Spelling

SCALES WITH ROOT = A

MAJOR TYPES

IONIAN (MAJOR)

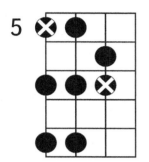
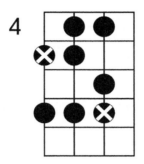
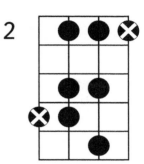

FIG.17 - IONIAN BEGINNING ON 4TH STRING

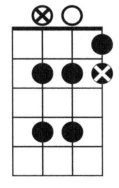
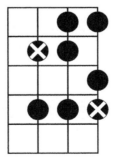
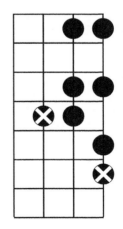

FIG.18 - IONIAN BEGINNING ON 3RD STRING

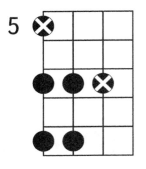
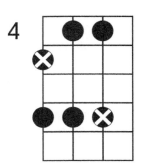
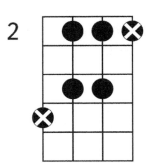

FIG.19 - MAJOR PENTATONIC BEGINNING ON 4TH STRING

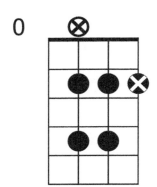
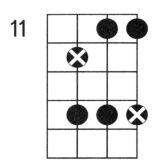
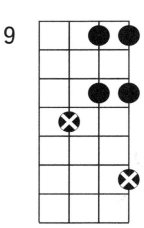

FIG.20 - MAJOR PENTATONIC BEGINNING ON 3RD STRING

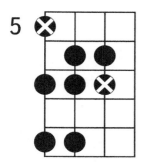

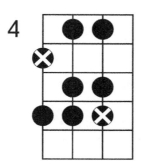

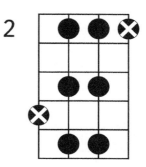

FIG.21 - LYDIAN BEGINNING ON 4TH STRING

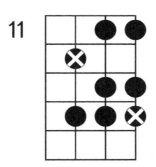

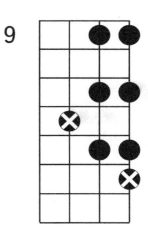

FIG.22 - LYDIAN BEGINNING ON 3RD STRING

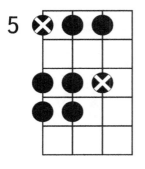
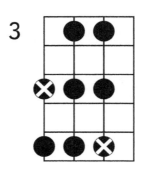
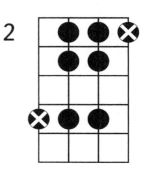

FIG.23 - AEOLIAN BEGINNING ON 4TH STRING

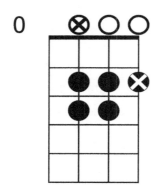
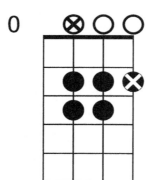
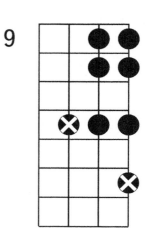

FIG.24 - AEOLIAN BEGINNING ON 3RD STRING

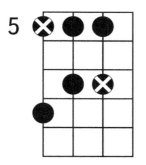 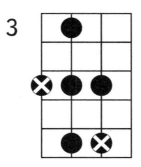 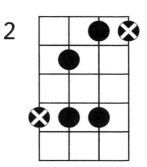

Fig.25 - Minor Pentatonic Beginning on 4th String

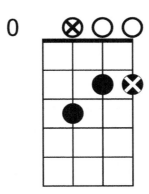 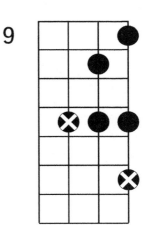

Fig.26 - Minor Pentatonic Beginning on 3rd String

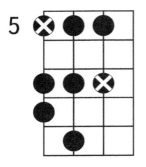

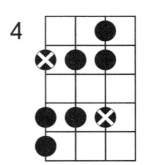

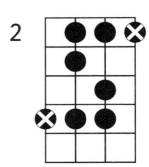

FIG.27 - DORIAN BEGINNING ON 4TH STRING

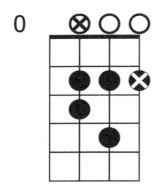

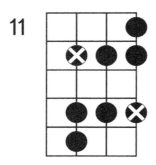

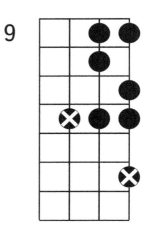

FIG.28 - DORIAN BEGINNING ON 3RD STRING

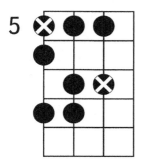
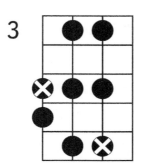
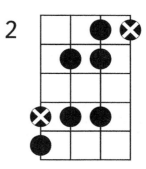

FIG.29 - PHRYGIAN BEGINNING ON 4TH STRING

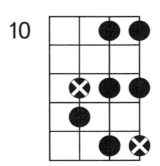
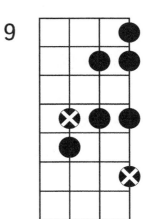

FIG.30 - PHRYGIAN BEGINNING ON 3RD STRING

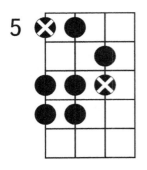

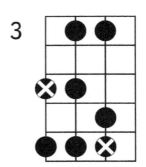

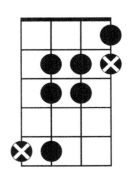

FIG.31 - HARMONIC BEGINNING ON 4TH STRING

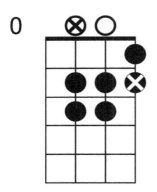

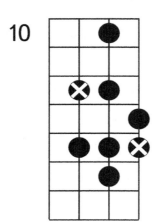

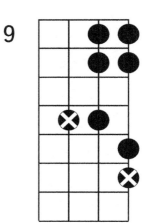

FIG.32 - HARMONIC BEGINNING ON 3RD STRING

Note: For Descending Melodic Minor, see Aeolian

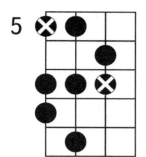
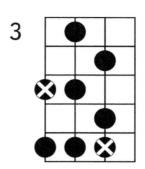
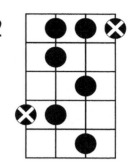

FIG.33 - MELODIC MINOR ASCENDING BEGINNING ON 4TH STRING

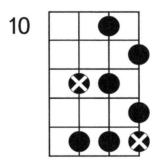
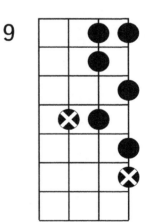

FIG.34 - MELODIC MINOR ASCENDING BEGINNING ON 3RD STRING

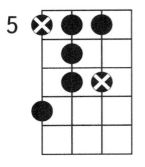
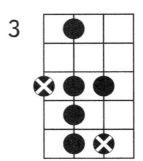
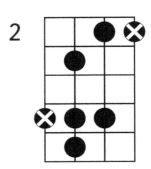

FIG.35 - BLUES SCALE BEGINNING ON 4TH STRING

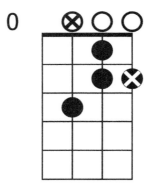
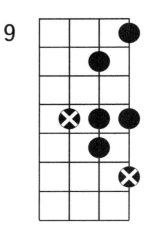

FIG.36 - BLUES SCALE BEGINNING ON 3RD STRING

DOMINANT TYPES

MIXOLYDIAN

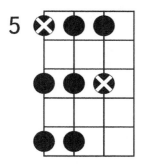 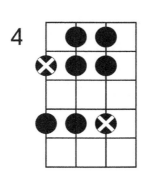 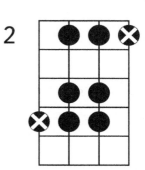

FIG.37 - MIXOLYDIAN BEGINNING ON 4TH STRING

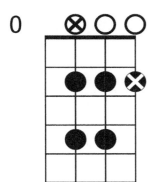 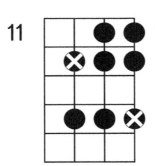 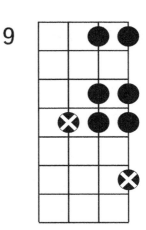

FIG.38 - MIXOLYDIAN BEGINNING ON 3RD STRING

AUGMENTED TYPES

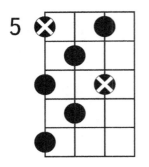 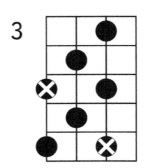 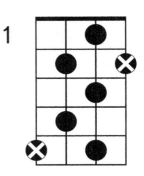

FIG.39 - WHOLE TONE BEGINNING ON 4TH STRING

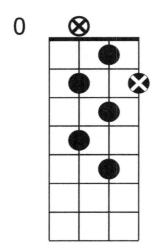 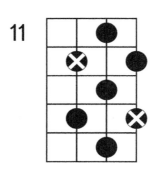 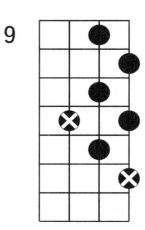

FIG.40 - WHOLE TONE BEGINNING ON 3RD STRING

DIMINISHED TYPES

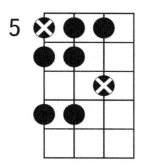
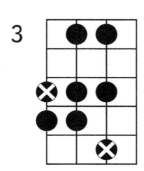
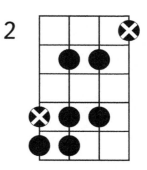

FIG.41 - LOCRIAN BEGINNING ON 4TH STRING

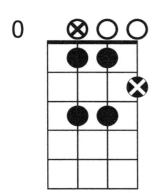
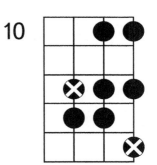

FIG.42 - LOCRIAN BEGINNING ON 3RD STRING

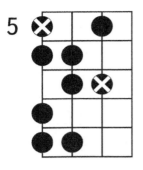

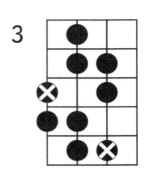

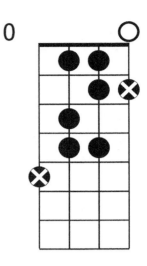

FIG.43 - HALF/WHOLE DIMINISHED BEGINNING ON 4TH STRING

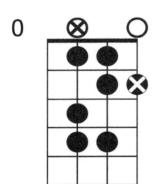

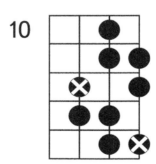

FIG.44 - HALF/WHOLE DIMINISHED BEGINNING ON 3RD STRING

SCALES WITH ROOT = A SHARP/B FLAT

MAJOR TYPES

IONIAN (MAJOR)

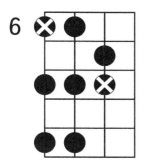

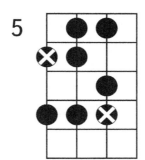

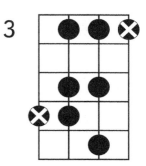

FIG.45 - IONIAN BEGINNING ON 4TH STRING

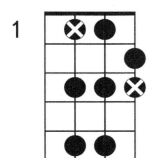

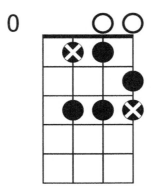

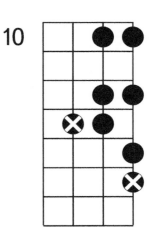

FIG.46 - IONIAN BEGINNING ON 3RD STRING

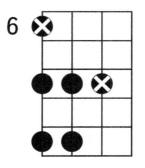
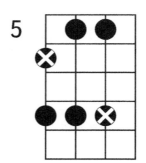
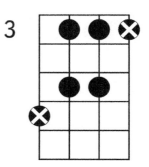

FIG.47 - MAJOR PENTATONIC BEGINNING ON 4TH STRING

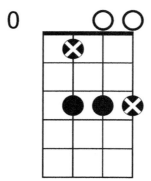
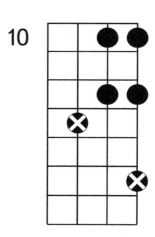

FIG.48 - MAJOR PENTATONIC BEGINNING ON 3RD STRING

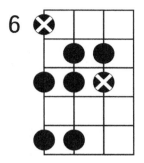
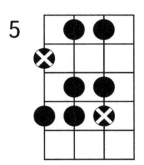
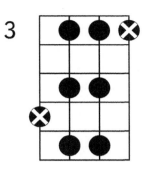

FIG.49 - LYDIAN BEGINNING ON 4TH STRING

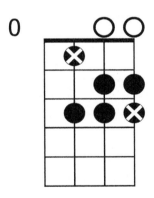
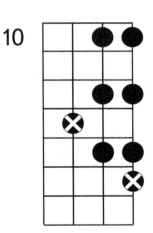

FIG.50 - LYDIAN BEGINNING ON 3RD STRING

AEOLIAN (NATURAL MINOR)

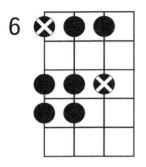
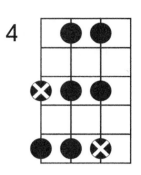
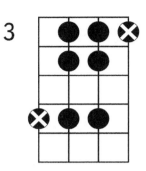

FIG.51 - AEOLIAN BEGINNING ON 4TH STRING

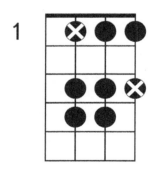
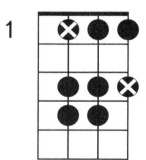
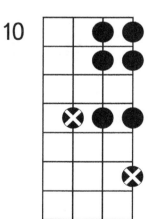

FIG.52 - AEOLIAN BEGINNING ON 3RD STRING

6 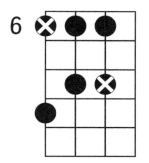   4 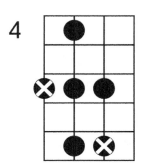   3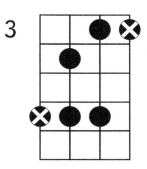

FIG.53 - MINOR PENTATONIC BEGINNING ON 4TH STRING

1   1   10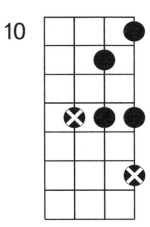

FIG.54 - MINOR PENTATONIC BEGINNING ON 3RD STRING

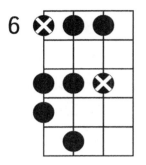 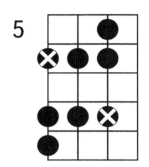 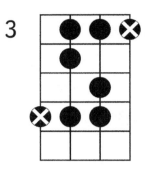

FIG.55 - DORIAN BEGINNING ON 4TH STRING

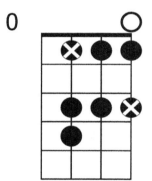 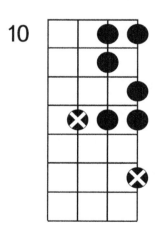

FIG.56 - DORIAN BEGINNING ON 3RD STRING

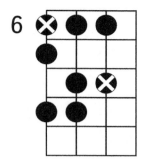
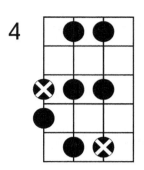
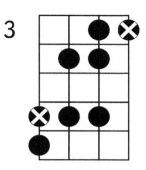

FIG.57 - PHRYGIAN BEGINNING ON 4TH STRING

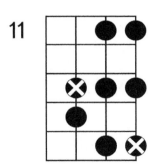
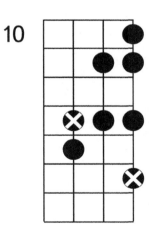

FIG.58 - PHRYGIAN BEGINNING ON 3RD STRING

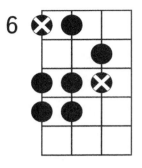

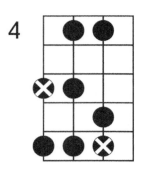

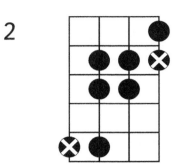

FIG.59 - HARMONIC BEGINNING ON 4TH STRING

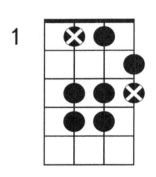

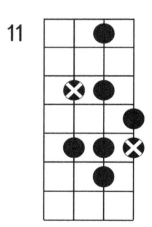

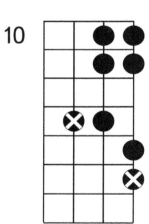

FIG.60 - HARMONIC BEGINNING ON 3RD STRING

Note: For Descending Melodic Minor, see Aeolian

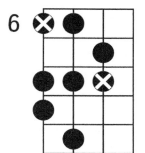
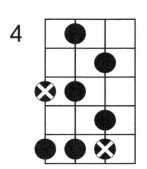
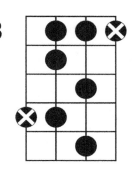

FIG.61 - MELODIC MINOR ASCENDING BEGINNING ON 4TH STRING

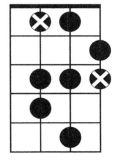
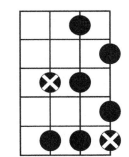
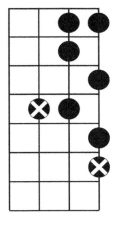

FIG.62 - MELODIC MINOR ASCENDING BEGINNING ON 3RD STRING

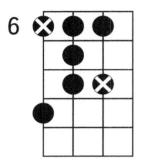
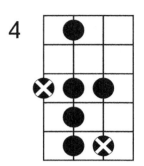
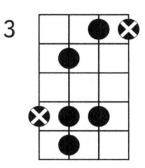

FIG.63 - BLUES SCALE BEGINNING ON 4TH STRING

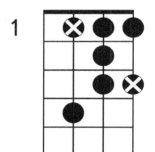
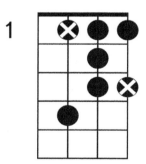
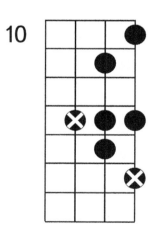

FIG.64 - BLUES SCALE BEGINNING ON 3RD STRING

MIXOLYDIAN

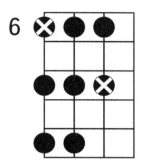 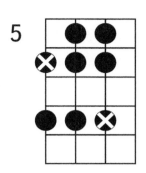 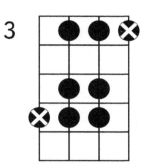

FIG.65 - MIXOLYDIAN BEGINNING ON 4TH STRING

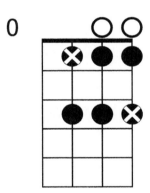 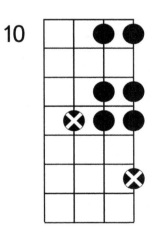

FIG.66 - MIXOLYDIAN BEGINNING ON 3RD STRING

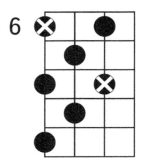

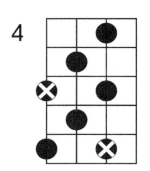

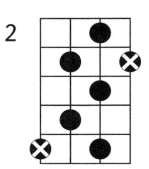

FIG.67 - WHOLE TONE BEGINNING ON 4TH STRING

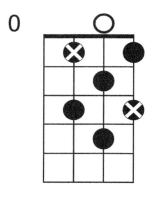

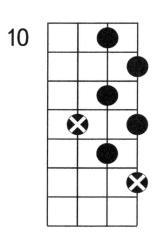

FIG.68 - WHOLE TONE BEGINNING ON 3RD STRING

38 BASS GUITAR SCALES ENCYCLOPEDIA: FROM SEEING MUSIC METHOD BOOKS

DIMINISHED TYPES

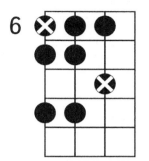 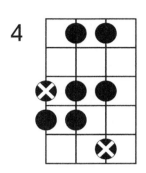 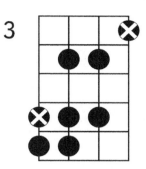

FIG.69 - LOCRIAN BEGINNING ON 4TH STRING

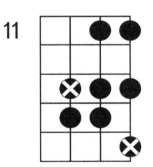

FIG.70 - LOCRIAN BEGINNING ON 3RD STRING

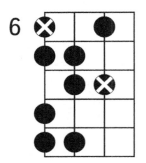
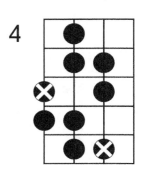
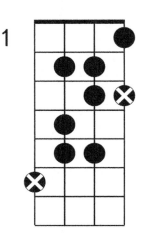

FIG.71 - HALF/WHOLE DIMINISHED BEGINNING ON 4TH STRING

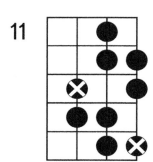

FIG.72 - HALF/WHOLE DIMINISHED BEGINNING ON 3RD STRING

SCALES WITH ROOT = B

MAJOR TYPES

IONIAN (MAJOR)

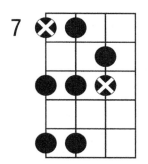
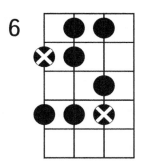
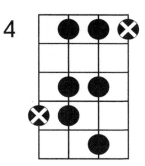

FIG.73 - IONIAN BEGINNING ON 4TH STRING

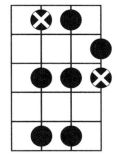
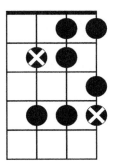
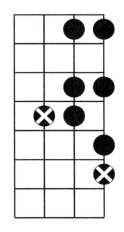

FIG.74 - IONIAN BEGINNING ON 3RD STRING

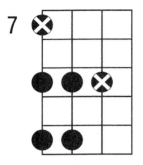
7

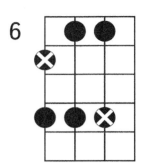
6

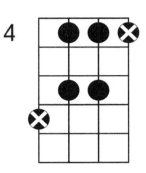
4

FIG.75 - MAJOR PENTATONIC BEGINNING ON 4TH STRING

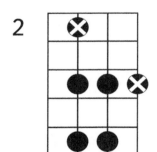
2

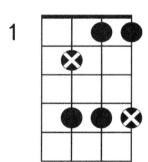
1

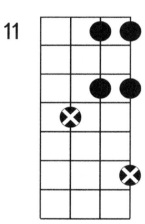
11

FIG.76 - MAJOR PENTATONIC BEGINNING ON 3RD STRING

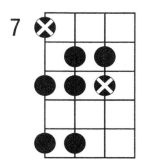

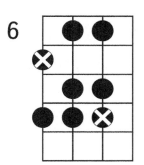

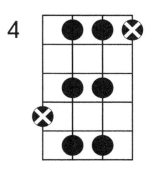

FIG.77 - LYDIAN BEGINNING ON 4TH STRING

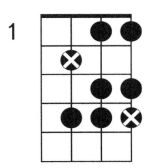

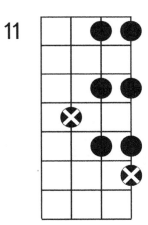

FIG.78 - LYDIAN BEGINNING ON 3RD STRING

AEOLIAN (NATURAL MINOR)

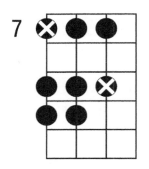 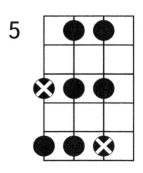 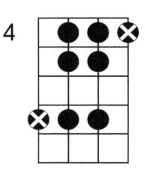

FIG.79 - AEOLIAN BEGINNING ON 4TH STRING

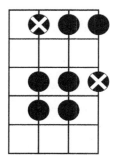 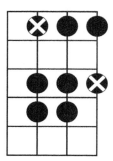 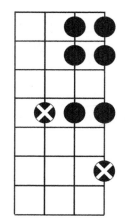

FIG.80 - AEOLIAN BEGINNING ON 3RD STRING

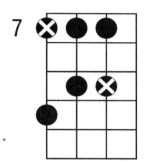 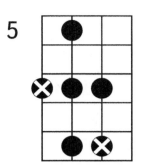 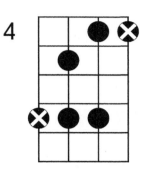

FIG.81 - MINOR PENTATONIC BEGINNING ON 4TH STRING

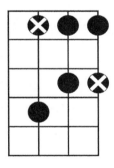 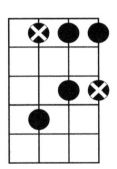 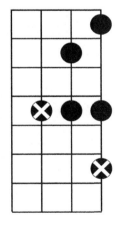

FIG.82 - MINOR PENTATONIC BEGINNING ON 3RD STRING

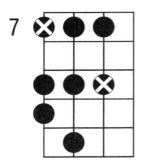 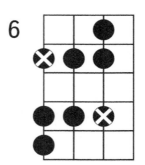 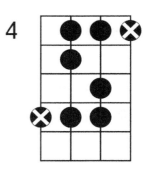

FIG.83 - DORIAN BEGINNING ON 4TH STRING

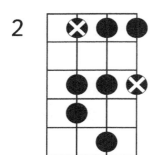 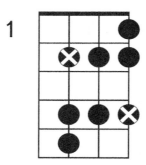 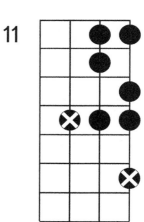

FIG.84 - DORIAN BEGINNING ON 3RD STRING

7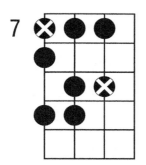

5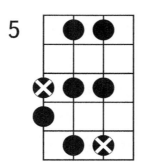

4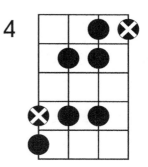

FIG.85 - PHRYGIAN BEGINNING ON 4TH STRING

2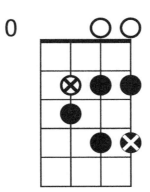

0

11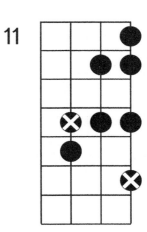

FIG.86 - PHRYGIAN BEGINNING ON 3RD STRING

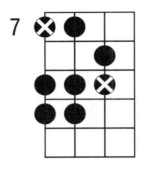
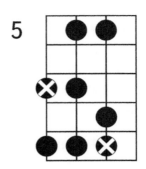
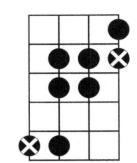

FIG.87 - HARMONIC BEGINNING ON 4TH STRING

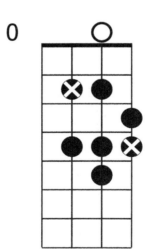
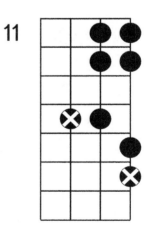

FIG.88 - HARMONIC BEGINNING ON 3RD STRING

Note: For Descending Melodic Minor, see Aeolian

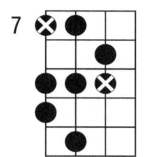 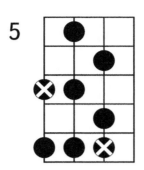 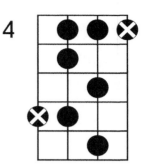

FIG.89 - MELODIC MINOR ASCENDING BEGINNING ON 4TH STRING

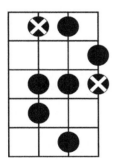 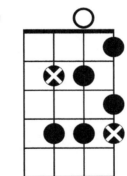 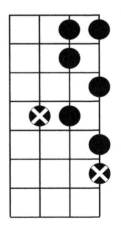

FIG.90 - MELODIC MINOR ASCENDING BEGINNING ON 3RD STRING

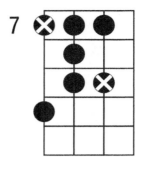
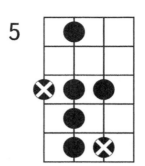
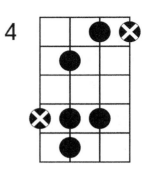

FIG.91 - BLUES SCALE BEGINNING ON 4TH STRING

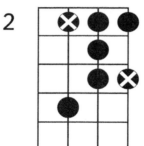
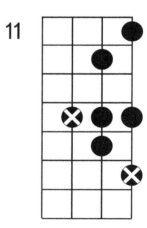

FIG.92 - BLUES SCALE BEGINNING ON 3RD STRING

DOMINANT TYPES

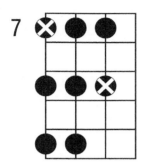
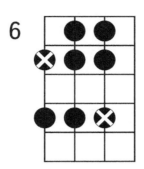
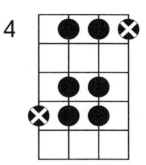

FIG.93 - MIXOLYDIAN BEGINNING ON 4TH STRING

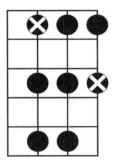
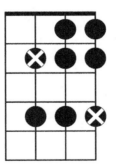
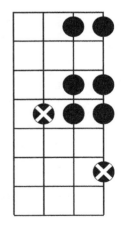

FIG.94 - MIXOLYDIAN BEGINNING ON 3RD STRING

AUGMENTED TYPES

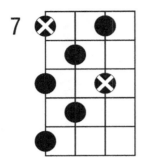
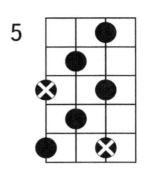
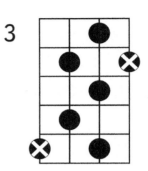

FIG.95 - WHOLE TONE BEGINNING ON 4TH STRING

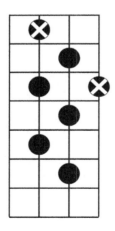
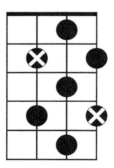
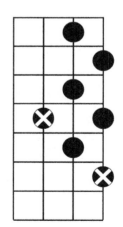

FIG.96 - WHOLE TONE BEGINNING ON 3RD STRING

DIMINISHED TYPES

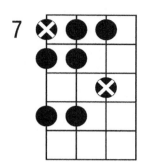 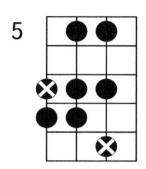 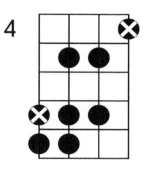

FIG.97 - LOCRIAN BEGINNING ON 4TH STRING

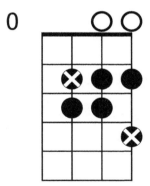

FIG.98 - LOCRIAN BEGINNING ON 3RD STRING

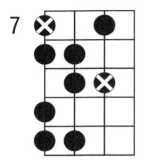 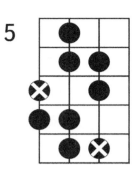 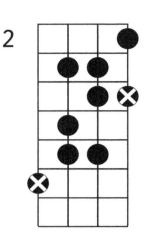

FIG.99 - HALF/WHOLE DIMINISHED BEGINNING ON 4TH STRING

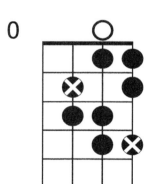

FIG.100 - HALF/WHOLE DIMINISHED BEGINNING ON 3RD STRING

SCALES WITH ROOT = C

MAJOR TYPES

IONIAN (MAJOR)

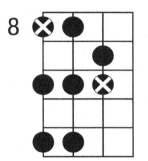
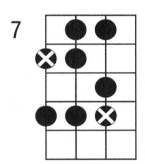
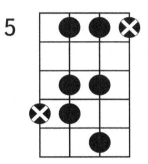

FIG.101 - IONIAN BEGINNING ON 4TH STRING

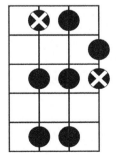
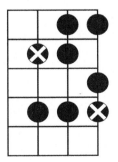
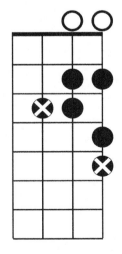

FIG.102 - IONIAN BEGINNING ON 3RD STRING

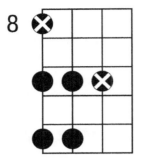
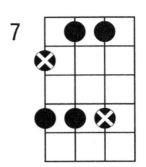
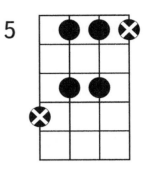

FIG.103 - MAJOR PENTATONIC BEGINNING ON 4TH STRING

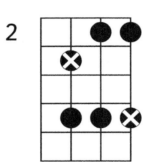
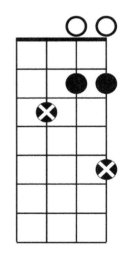

FIG.104 - MAJOR PENTATONIC BEGINNING ON 3RD STRING

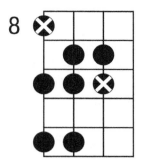

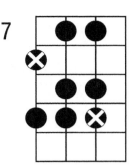

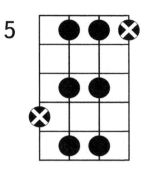

FIG.105 - LYDIAN BEGINNING ON 4TH STRING

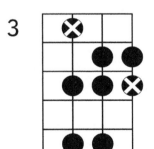

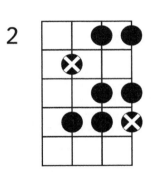

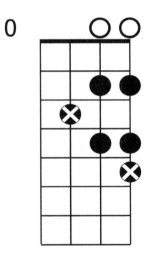

FIG.106 - LYDIAN BEGINNING ON 3RD STRING

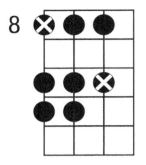
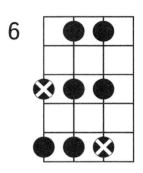
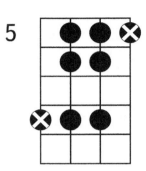

FIG.107 - AEOLIAN BEGINNING ON 4TH STRING

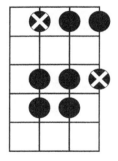
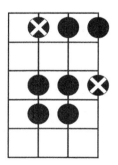
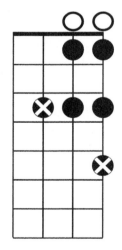

FIG.108 - AEOLIAN BEGINNING ON 3RD STRING

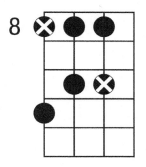
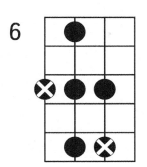
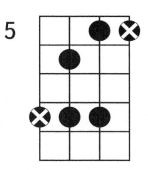

FIG.109 - MINOR PENTATONIC BEGINNING ON 4TH STRING

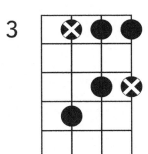
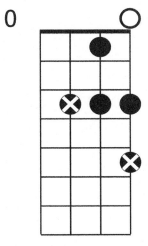

FIG.110 - MINOR PENTATONIC BEGINNING ON 3RD STRING

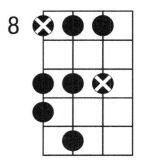
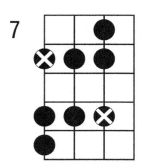
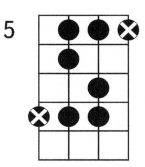

FIG.111 - DORIAN BEGINNING ON 4TH STRING

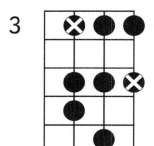
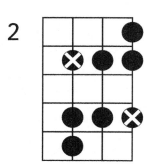
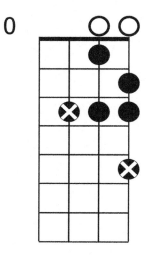

FIG.112 - DORIAN BEGINNING ON 3RD STRING

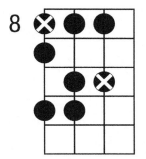 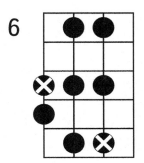 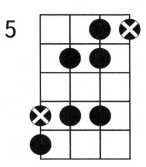

FIG.113 - PHRYGIAN BEGINNING ON 4TH STRING

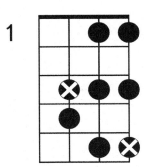 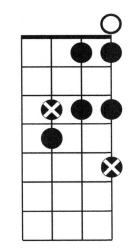

FIG.114 - PHRYGIAN BEGINNING ON 3RD STRING

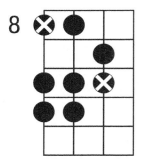
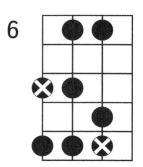
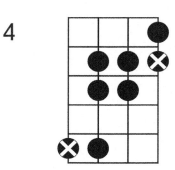

FIG.115 - HARMONIC BEGINNING ON 4TH STRING

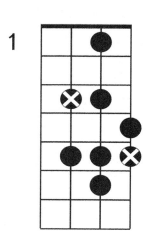
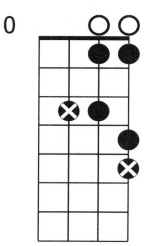

FIG.116 - HARMONIC BEGINNING ON 3RD STRING

Note: For Descending Melodic Minor, see Aeolian

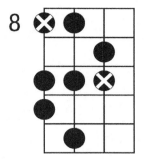 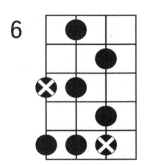 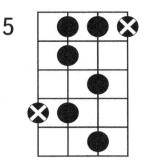

FIG.117 - MELODIC MINOR ASCENDING BEGINNING ON 4TH STRING

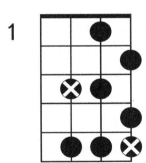 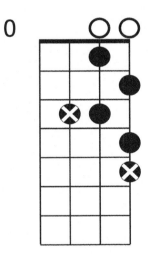

FIG.118 - MELODIC MINOR ASCENDING BEGINNING ON 3RD STRING

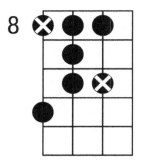
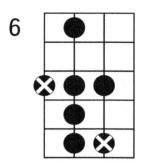
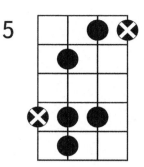

FIG.119 - BLUES SCALE BEGINNING ON 4TH STRING

FIG.119 - BLUES SCALE BEGINNING ON 4TH STRING

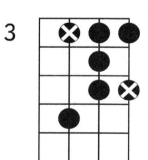
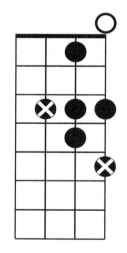

FIG.120 - BLUES SCALE BEGINNING ON 3RD STRING

8 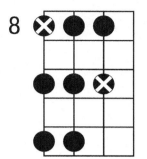   7 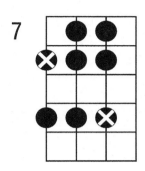   5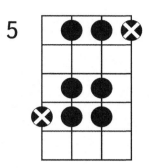

FIG.121 - MIXOLYDIAN BEGINNING ON 4TH STRING

3 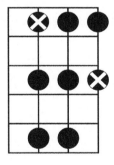   2 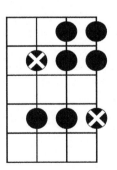   0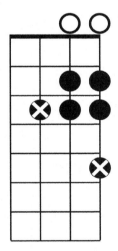

FIG.122 - MIXOLYDIAN BEGINNING ON 3RD STRING

AUGMENTED TYPES

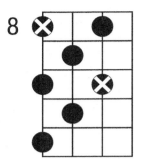
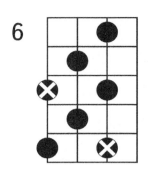
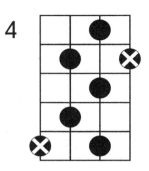

FIG.123 - WHOLE TONE BEGINNING ON 4TH STRING

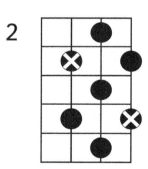
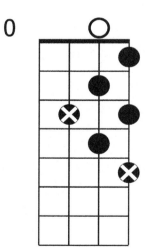

FIG.124 - WHOLE TONE BEGINNING ON 3RD STRING

66 BASS GUITAR SCALES ENCYCLOPEDIA: FROM SEEING MUSIC METHOD BOOKS

DIMINISHED TYPES

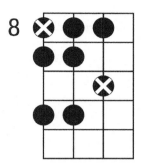 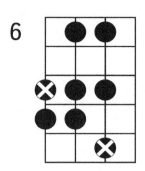 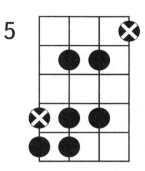

FIG.125 - LOCRIAN BEGINNING ON 4TH STRING

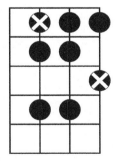 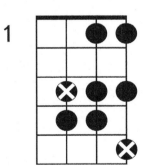

FIG.126 - LOCRIAN BEGINNING ON 3RD STRING

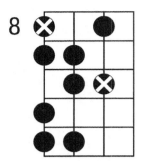 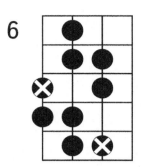 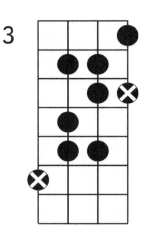

FIG.127 - HALF/WHOLE DIMINISHED BEGINNING ON 4TH STRING

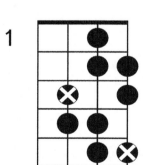

FIG.128 - HALF/WHOLE DIMINISHED BEGINNING ON 3RD STRING

SCALES WITH ROOT = C SHARP/D FLAT

MAJOR TYPES

IONIAN (MAJOR)

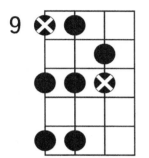

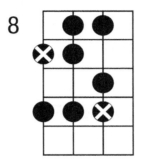

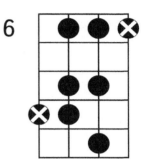

FIG.129 - IONIAN BEGINNING ON 4TH STRING

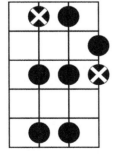

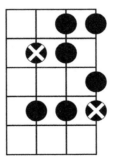

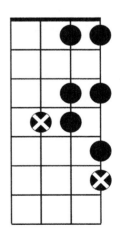

FIG.130 - IONIAN BEGINNING ON 3RD STRING

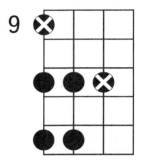 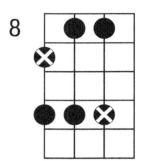 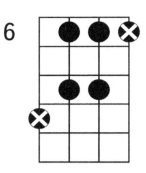

FIG.131 - MAJOR PENTATONIC BEGINNING ON 4TH STRING

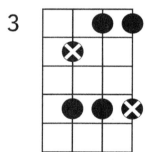 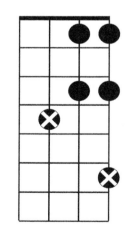

FIG.132 - MAJOR PENTATONIC BEGINNING ON 3RD STRING

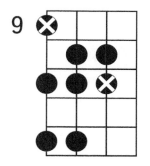
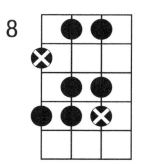
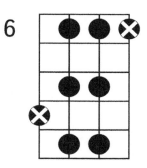

FIG.133 - LYDIAN BEGINNING ON 4TH STRING

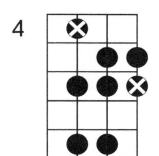
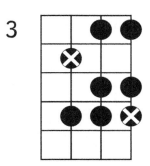
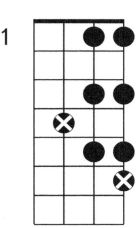

FIG.134 - LYDIAN BEGINNING ON 3RD STRING

AEOLIAN (NATURAL MINOR)

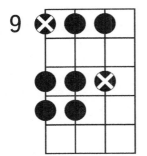
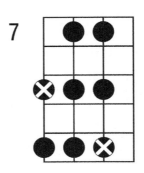
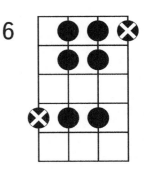

FIG.135 - AEOLIAN BEGINNING ON 4TH STRING

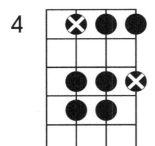
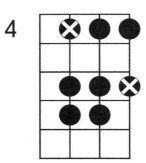
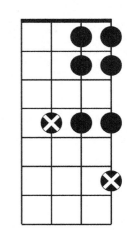

FIG.136 - AEOLIAN BEGINNING ON 3RD STRING

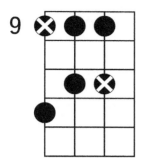

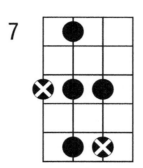

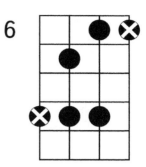

FIG.137 - MINOR PENTATONIC BEGINNING ON 4TH STRING

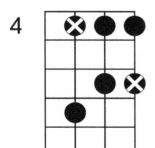

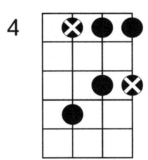

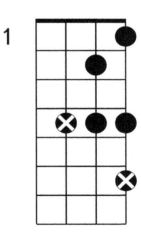

FIG.138 - MINOR PENTATONIC BEGINNING ON 3RD STRING

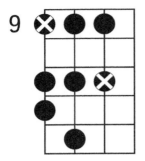 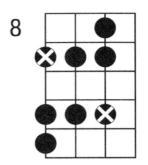 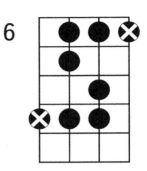

FIG.139 - DORIAN BEGINNING ON 4TH STRING

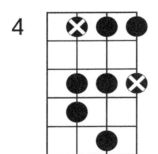 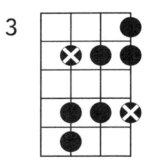 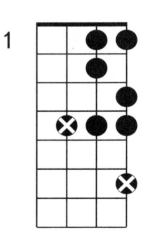

FIG.140 - DORIAN BEGINNING ON 3RD STRING

9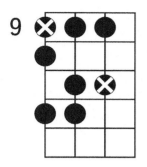

7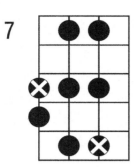

6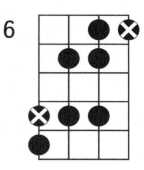

FIG.141 - PHRYGIAN BEGINNING ON 4TH STRING

4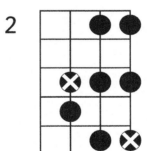

2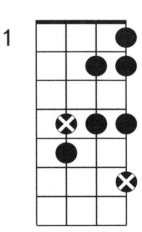

1

FIG.142 - PHRYGIAN BEGINNING ON 3RD STRING

9 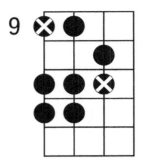 7 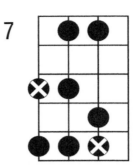 5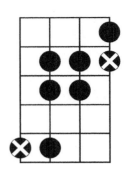

FIG.143 - HARMONIC BEGINNING ON 4TH STRING

4 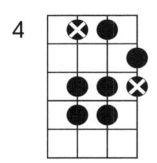 2 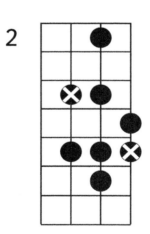 1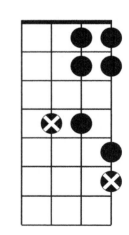

FIG.144 - HARMONIC BEGINNING ON 3RD STRING

Note: For Descending Melodic Minor, see Aeolian

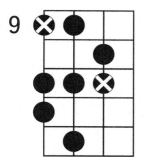 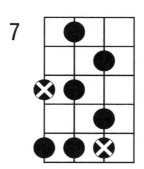 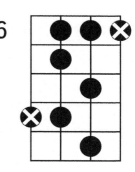

FIG.145 - MELODIC MINOR ASCENDING BEGINNING ON 4TH STRING

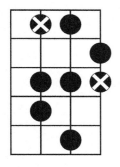 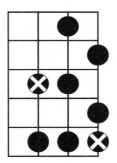 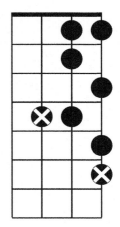

FIG.146 - MELODIC MINOR ASCENDING BEGINNING ON 3RD STRING

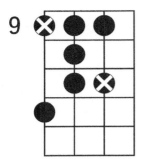

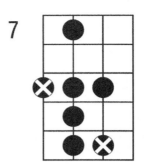

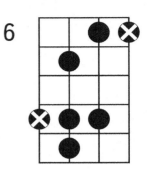

FIG.147 - BLUES SCALE BEGINNING ON 4TH STRING

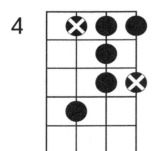

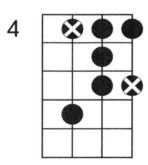

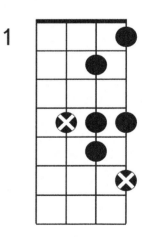

FIG.148 - BLUES SCALE BEGINNING ON 3RD STRING

DOMINANT TYPES

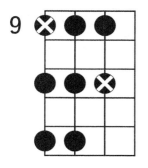

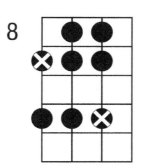

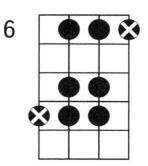

FIG.149 - MIXOLYDIAN BEGINNING ON 4TH STRING

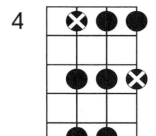

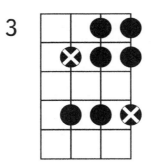

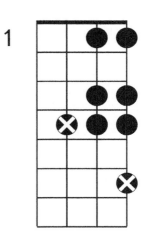

FIG.150 - MIXOLYDIAN BEGINNING ON 3RD STRING

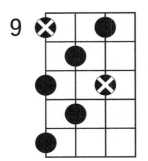
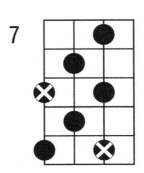
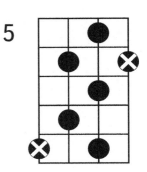

FIG.151 - WHOLE TONE BEGINNING ON 4TH STRING

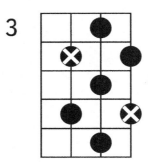
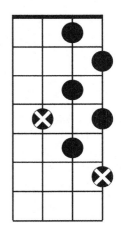

FIG.152 - WHOLE TONE BEGINNING ON 3RD STRING

DIMINISHED TYPES

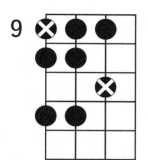
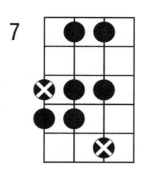
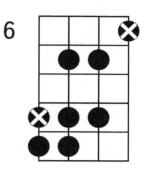

FIG.153 - LOCRIAN BEGINNING ON 4TH STRING

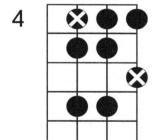
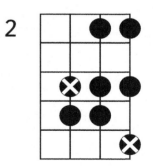

FIG.154 - LOCRIAN BEGINNING ON 3RD STRING

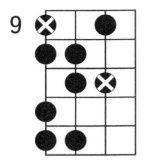 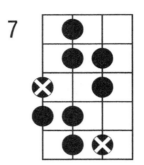 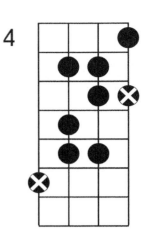

FIG.155 - HALF/WHOLE DIMINISHED BEGINNING ON 4TH STRING

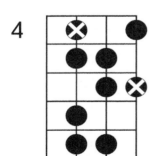 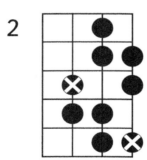

FIG.156 - HALF/WHOLE DIMINISHED BEGINNING ON 3RD STRING

SCALES WITH ROOT = D

MAJOR TYPES

IONIAN (MAJOR)

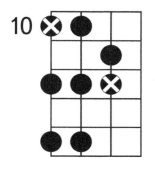
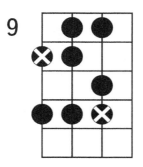
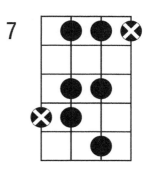

FIG.157 - IONIAN BEGINNING ON 4TH STRING

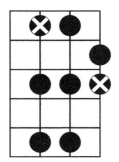
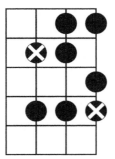
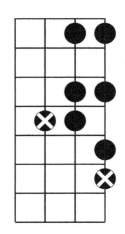

FIG.158 - IONIAN BEGINNING ON 3RD STRING

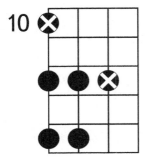 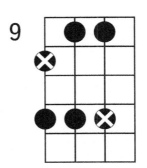 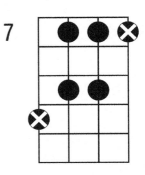

FIG.159 - MAJOR PENTATONIC BEGINNING ON 4TH STRING

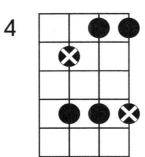 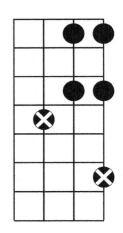

FIG.160 - MAJOR PENTATONIC BEGINNING ON 3RD STRING

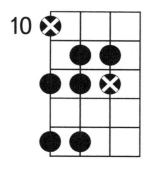

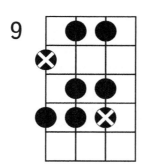

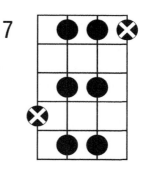

FIG.161 - LYDIAN BEGINNING ON 4TH STRING

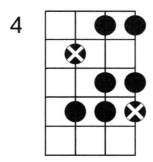

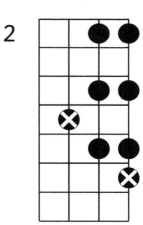

FIG.162 - LYDIAN BEGINNING ON 3RD STRING

MINOR TYPES
AEOLIAN (NATURAL MINOR)

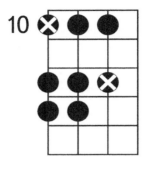

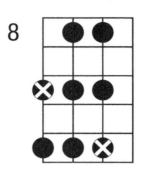

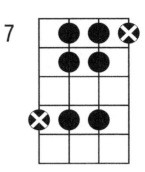

FIG.163 - AEOLIAN BEGINNING ON 4TH STRING

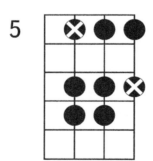

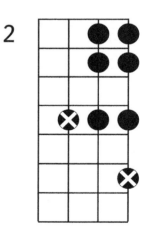

FIG.164 - AEOLIAN BEGINNING ON 3RD STRING

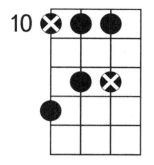
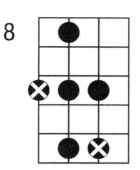
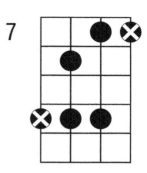

FIG.165 - MINOR PENTATONIC BEGINNING ON 4TH STRING

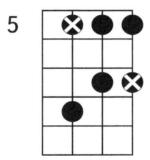
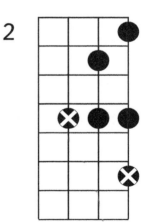

FIG.166 - MINOR PENTATONIC BEGINNING ON 3RD STRING

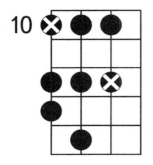 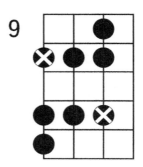 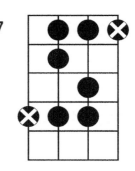

FIG.167 - DORIAN BEGINNING ON 4TH STRING

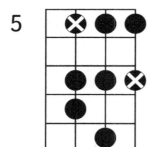 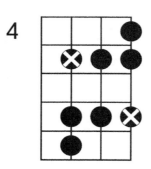 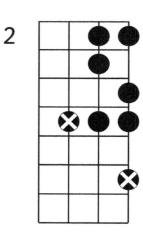

FIG.168 - DORIAN BEGINNING ON 3RD STRING

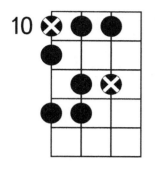
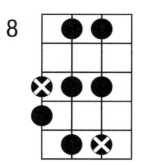
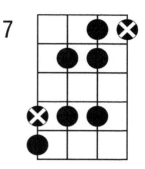

FIG.169 - PHRYGIAN BEGINNING ON 4TH STRING

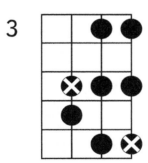
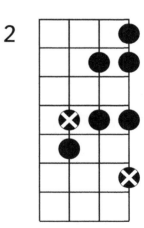

FIG.170 - PHRYGIAN BEGINNING ON 3RD STRING

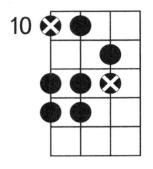

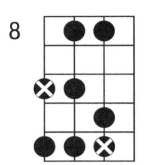

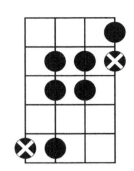

FIG.171 - HARMONIC BEGINNING ON 4TH STRING

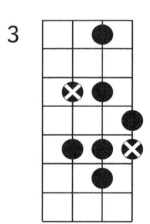

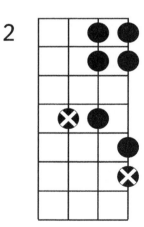

FIG.172 - HARMONIC BEGINNING ON 3RD STRING

Note: For Descending Melodic Minor, see Aeolian

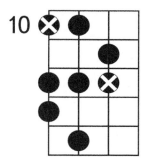 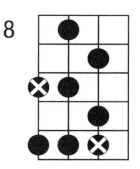 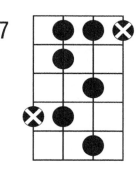

FIG.173 - MELODIC MINOR ASCENDING BEGINNING ON 4TH STRING

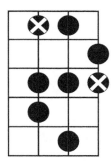 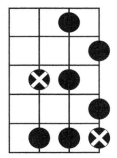 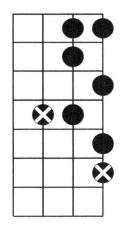

FIG.174 - MELODIC MINOR ASCENDING BEGINNING ON 3RD STRING

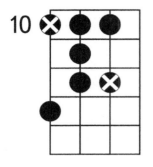
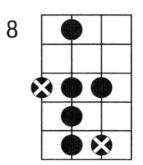
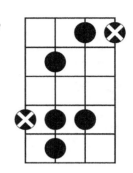

FIG.175 - BLUES SCALE BEGINNING ON 4TH STRING

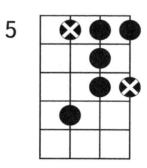
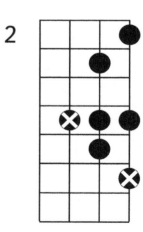

FIG.176 - BLUES SCALE BEGINNING ON 3RD STRING

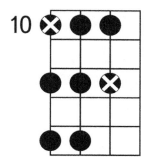

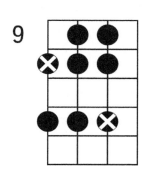

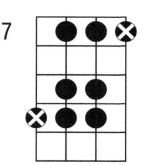

FIG.177 - MIXOLYDIAN BEGINNING ON 4TH STRING

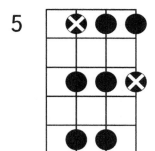

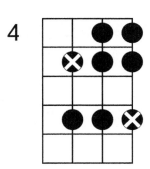

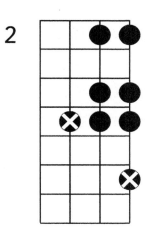

FIG.178 - MIXOLYDIAN BEGINNING ON 3RD STRING

AUGMENTED TYPES

WHOLE TONE

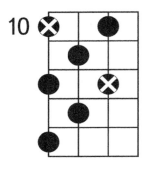

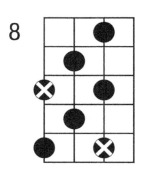

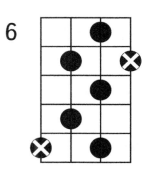

FIG.179 - WHOLE TONE BEGINNING ON 4TH STRING

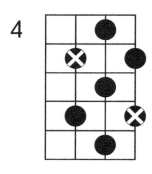

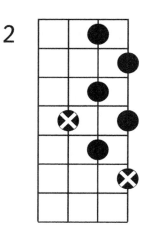

FIG.180 - WHOLE TONE BEGINNING ON 3RD STRING

DIMINISHED TYPES

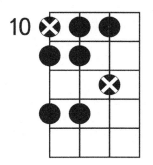
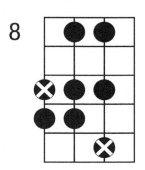
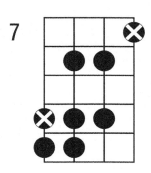

FIG.181 - LOCRIAN BEGINNING ON 4TH STRING

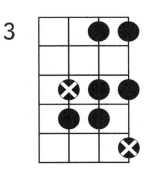

FIG.182 - LOCRIAN BEGINNING ON 3RD STRING

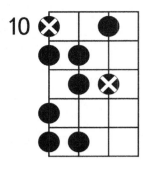
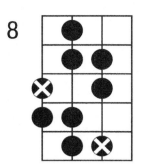
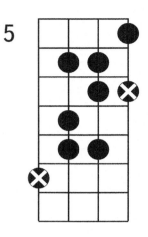

FIG.183 - HALF/WHOLE DIMINISHED BEGINNING ON 4TH STRING

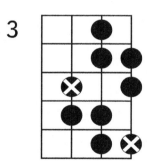

FIG.184 - HALF/WHOLE DIMINISHED BEGINNING ON 3RD STRING

SCALES WITH ROOT = D SHARP/E FLAT

MAJOR TYPES

IONIAN (MAJOR)

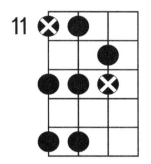
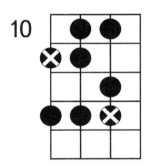
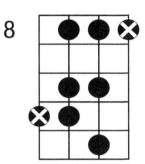

FIG.185 - IONIAN BEGINNING ON 4TH STRING

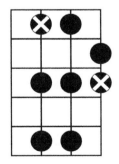
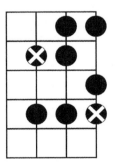
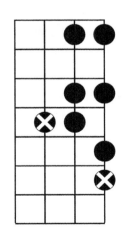

FIG.186 - IONIAN BEGINNING ON 3RD STRING

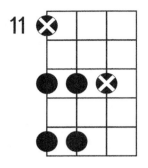

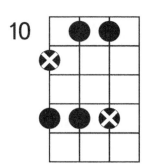

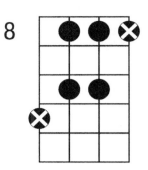

FIG.187 - MAJOR PENTATONIC BEGINNING ON 4TH STRING

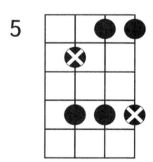

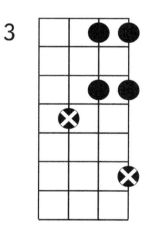

FIG.188 - MAJOR PENTATONIC BEGINNING ON 3RD STRING

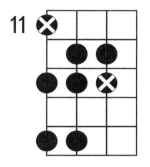
11

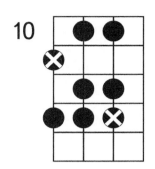
10

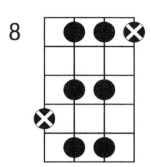
8

FIG.189 - LYDIAN BEGINNING ON 4TH STRING

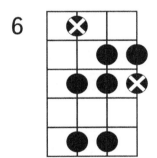
6

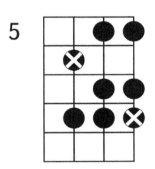
5

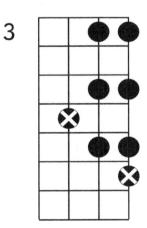
3

FIG.190 - LYDIAN BEGINNING ON 3RD STRING

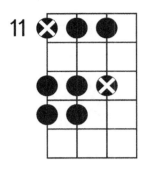
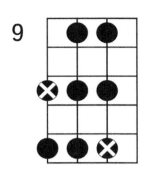
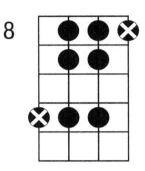

FIG.191 - AEOLIAN BEGINNING ON 4TH STRING

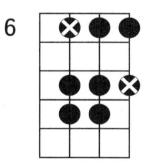
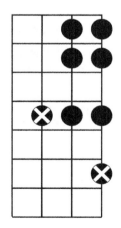

FIG.192 - AEOLIAN BEGINNING ON 3RD STRING

11 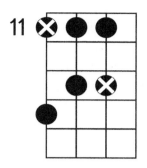   9 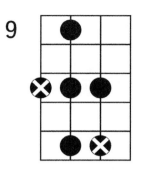   8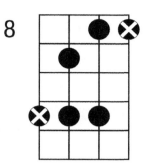

FIG.193 - MINOR PENTATONIC BEGINNING ON 4TH STRING

6 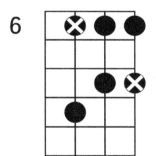   6 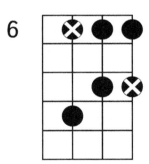   3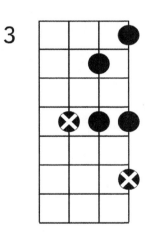

FIG.194 - MINOR PENTATONIC BEGINNING ON 3RD STRING

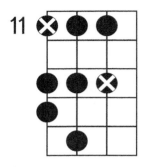

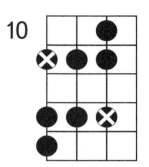

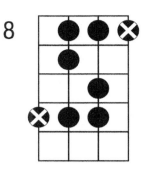

FIG.195 - DORIAN BEGINNING ON 4TH STRING

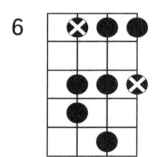

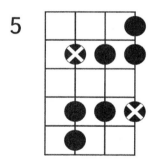

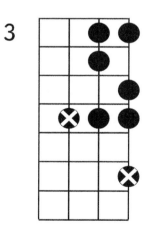

FIG.196 - DORIAN BEGINNING ON 3RD STRING

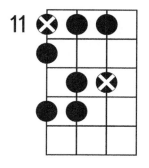
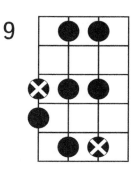
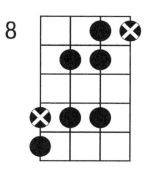

FIG.197 - PHRYGIAN BEGINNING ON 4TH STRING

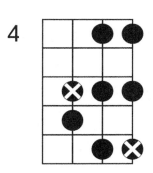
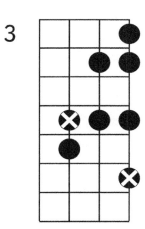

FIG.198 - PHRYGIAN BEGINNING ON 3RD STRING

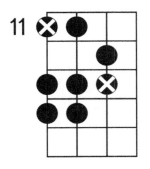
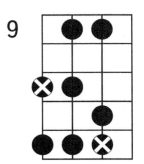
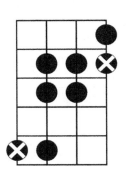

FIG.199 - HARMONIC BEGINNING ON 4TH STRING

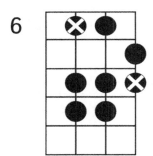
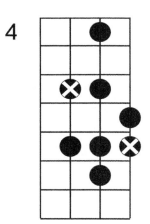
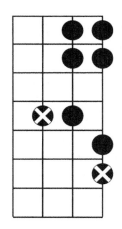

FIG.200 - HARMONIC BEGINNING ON 3RD STRING

Note: For Descending Melodic Minor, see Aeolian

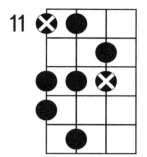 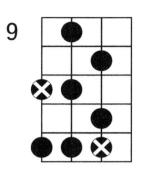 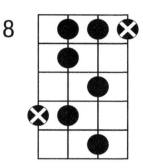

FIG.201 - MELODIC MINOR ASCENDING BEGINNING ON 4TH STRING

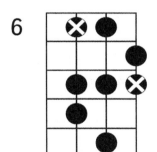 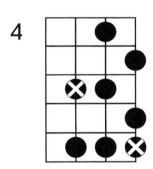 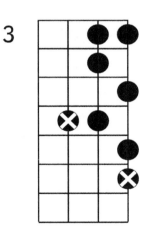

FIG.202 - MELODIC MINOR ASCENDING BEGINNING ON 3RD STRING

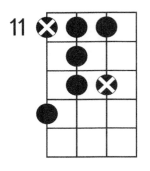

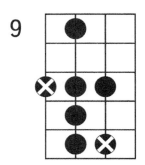

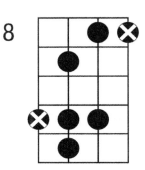

FIG.203 - BLUES SCALE BEGINNING ON 4TH STRING

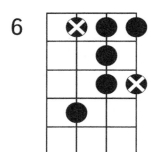

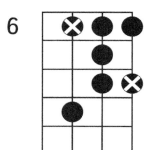

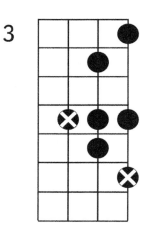

FIG.204 - BLUES SCALE BEGINNING ON 3RD STRING

DOMINANT TYPES

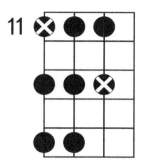
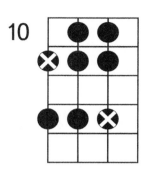
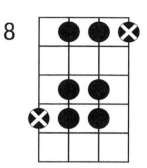

FIG.205 - MIXOLYDIAN BEGINNING ON 4TH STRING

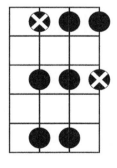
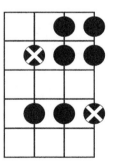
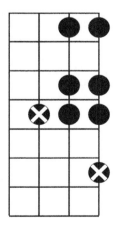

FIG.206 - MIXOLYDIAN BEGINNING ON 3RD STRING

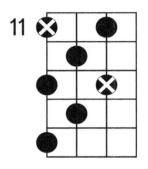
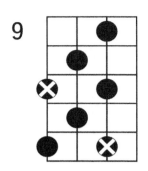
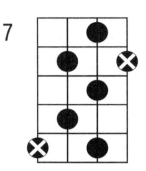

FIG.207 - WHOLE TONE BEGINNING ON 4TH STRING

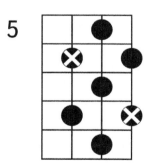
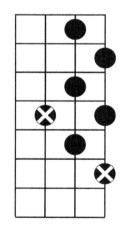

FIG.208 - WHOLE TONE BEGINNING ON 3RD STRING

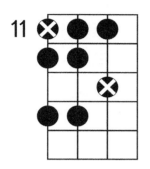
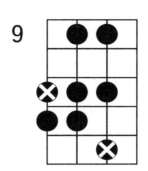
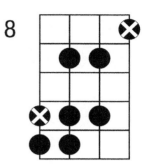

FIG.209 - LOCRIAN BEGINNING ON 4TH STRING

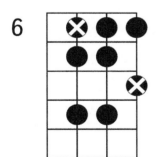
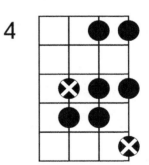

FIG.210 - LOCRIAN BEGINNING ON 3RD STRING

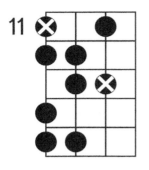 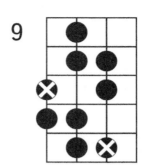 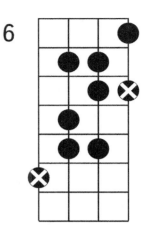

FIG.211 - HALF/WHOLE DIMINISHED BEGINNING ON 4TH STRING

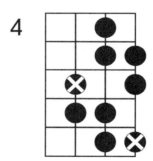

FIG.212 - HALF/WHOLE DIMINISHED BEGINNING ON 3RD STRING

SCALES WITH ROOT = E

MAJOR TYPES

IONIAN (MAJOR)

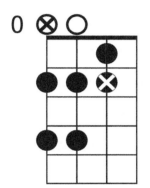

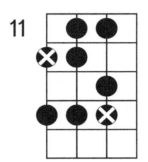

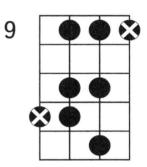

FIG.213 - Ionian Beginning on 4th String

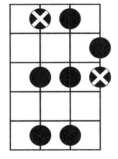

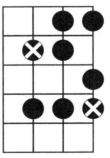

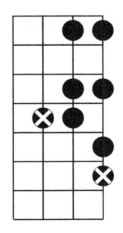

FIG.214 - Ionian Beginning on 3rd String

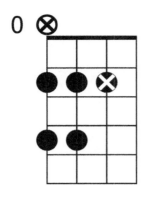
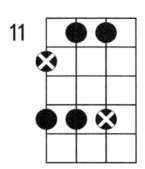
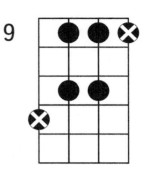

FIG.215 - MAJOR PENTATONIC BEGINNING ON 4TH STRING

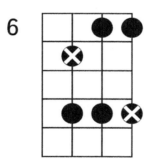
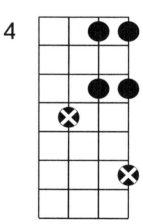

FIG.216 - MAJOR PENTATONIC BEGINNING ON 3RD STRING

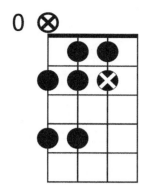

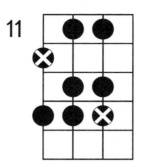

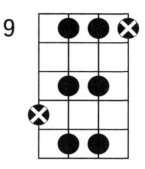

FIG.217 - LYDIAN BEGINNING ON 4TH STRING

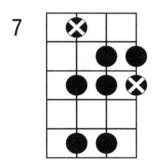

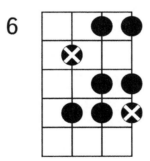

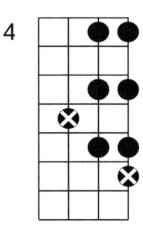

FIG.218 - LYDIAN BEGINNING ON 3RD STRING

AEOLIAN (NATURAL MINOR)

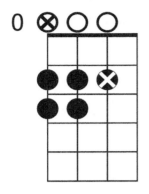

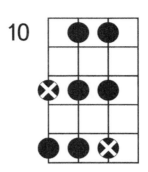

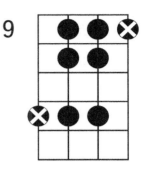

FIG.219 - AEOLIAN BEGINNING ON 4TH STRING

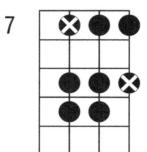

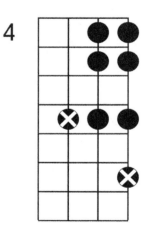

FIG.220 - AEOLIAN BEGINNING ON 3RD STRING

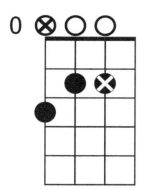

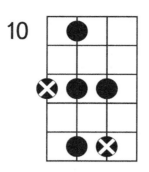

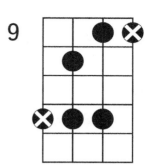

FIG.221 - MINOR PENTATONIC BEGINNING ON 4TH STRING

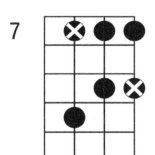

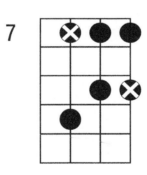

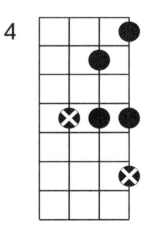

FIG.222 - MINOR PENTATONIC BEGINNING ON 3RD STRING

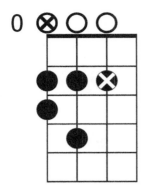
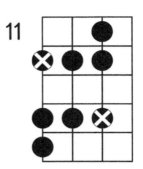
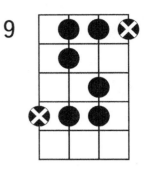

FIG.223 - DORIAN BEGINNING ON 4TH STRING

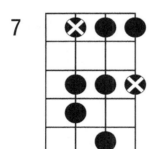
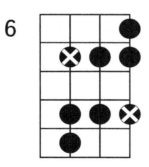
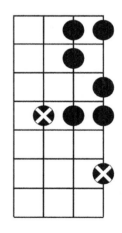

FIG.224 - DORIAN BEGINNING ON 3RD STRING

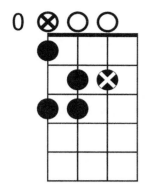 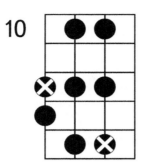 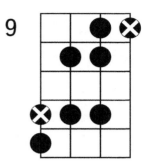

Fig.225 - Phrygian Beginning on 4th String

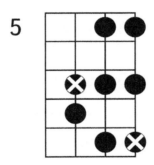 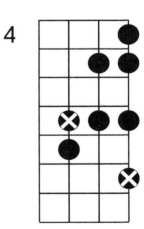

Fig.226 - Phrygian Beginning on 3rd String

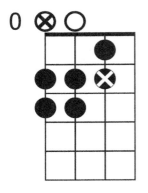

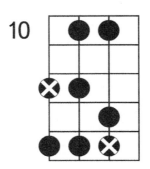

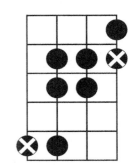

FIG.227 - HARMONIC BEGINNING ON 4TH STRING

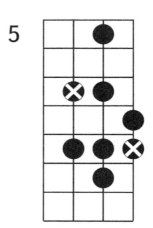

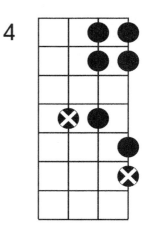

FIG.228 - HARMONIC BEGINNING ON 3RD STRING

Note: For Descending Melodic Minor, see Aeolian

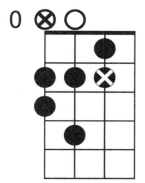

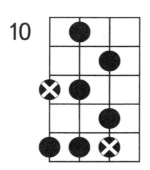

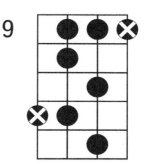

FIG.229 - MELODIC MINOR ASCENDING BEGINNING ON 4TH STRING

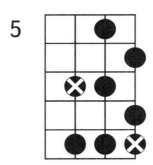

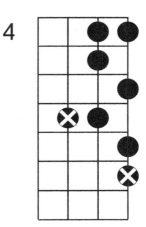

FIG.230 - MELODIC MINOR ASCENDING BEGINNING ON 3RD STRING

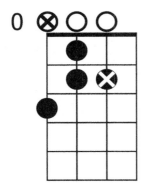 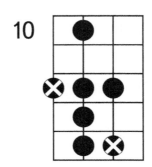 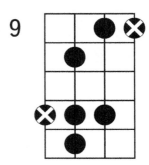

FIG.231 - BLUES SCALE BEGINNING ON 4TH STRING

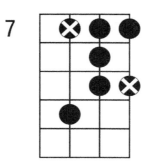 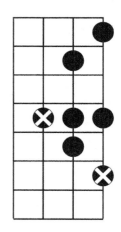

FIG.232 - BLUES SCALE BEGINNING ON 3RD STRING

DOMINANT TYPES

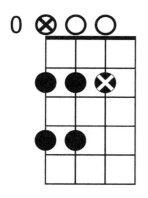

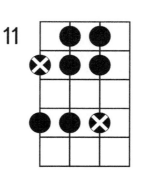

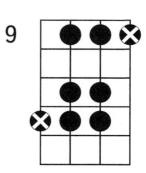

FIG.233 - MIXOLYDIAN BEGINNING ON 4TH STRING

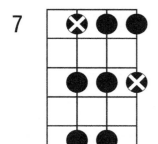

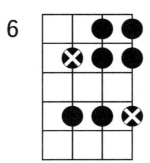

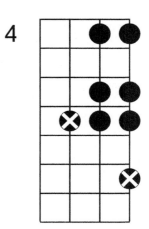

FIG.234 - MIXOLYDIAN BEGINNING ON 3RD STRING

AUGMENTED TYPES

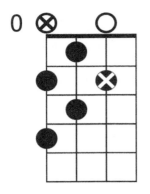
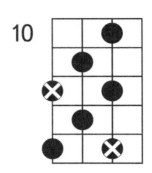
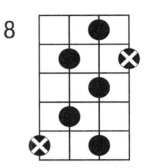

FIG.235 - WHOLE TONE BEGINNING ON 4TH STRING

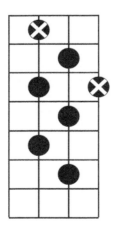
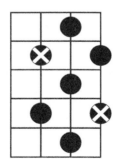
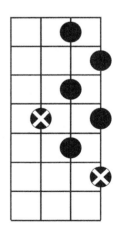

FIG.236 - WHOLE TONE BEGINNING ON 3RD STRING

DIMINISHED TYPES

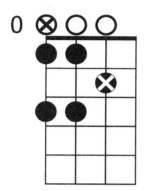
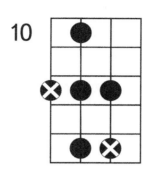
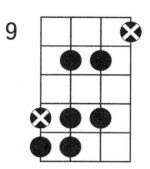

FIG.237 - LOCRIAN BEGINNING ON 4TH STRING

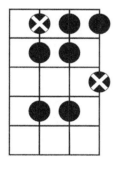
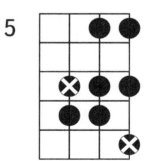

FIG.238 - LOCRIAN BEGINNING ON 3RD STRING

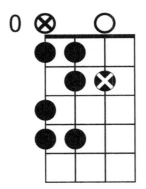
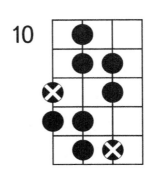
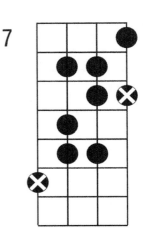

FIG.239 - HALF/WHOLE DIMINISHED BEGINNING ON 4TH STRING

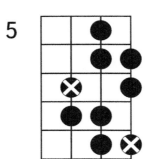

FIG.240 - HALF/WHOLE DIMINISHED BEGINNING ON 3RD STRING

SCALES WITH ROOT = F

MAJOR TYPES

IONIAN (MAJOR)

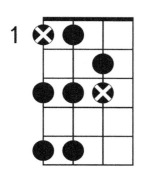

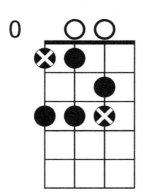

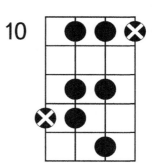

FIG.241 - IONIAN BEGINNING ON 4TH STRING

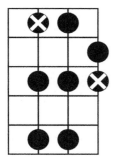

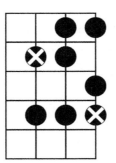

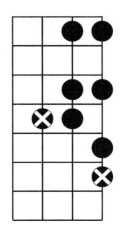

FIG.242 - IONIAN BEGINNING ON 3RD STRING

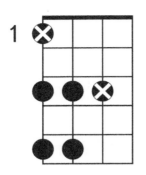

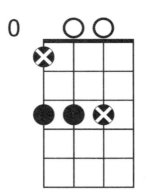

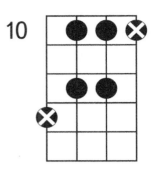

FIG.243 - MAJOR PENTATONIC BEGINNING ON 4TH STRING

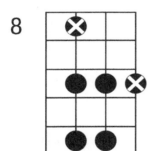

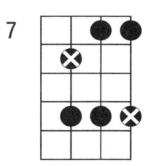

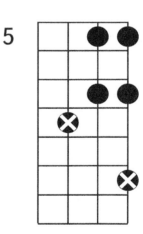

FIG.244 - MAJOR PENTATONIC BEGINNING ON 3RD STRING

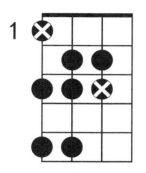
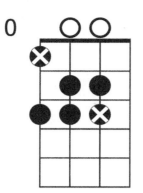
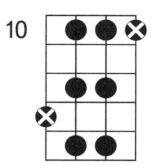

FIG.245 - Lᴏᴅɪᴀɴ Bᴇɢɪɴɴɪɴɢ ᴏɴ 4ᴛʜ Sᴛʀɪɴɢ

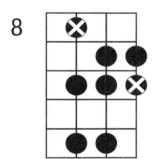
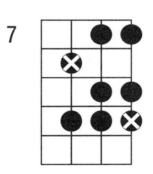
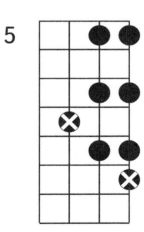

FIG.246 - Lᴏᴅɪᴀɴ Bᴇɢɪɴɴɪɴɢ ᴏɴ 3ʀᴅ Sᴛʀɪɴɢ

AEOLIAN (NATURAL MINOR)

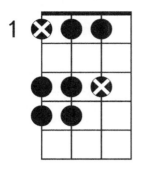

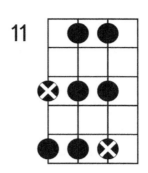

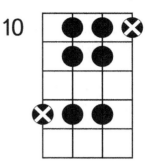

FIG.247 - Aeolian Beginning on 4th String

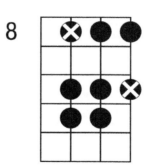

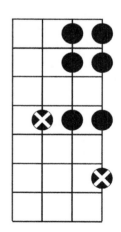

FIG.248 - Aeolian Beginning on 3rd String

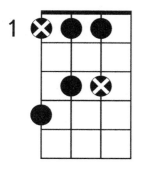
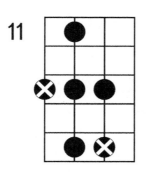
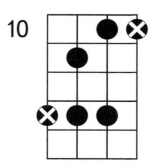

FIG.249 - MINOR PENTATONIC BEGINNING ON 4TH STRING

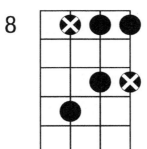
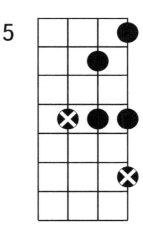

FIG.250 - MINOR PENTATONIC BEGINNING ON 3RD STRING

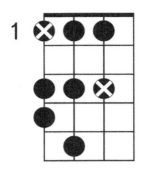
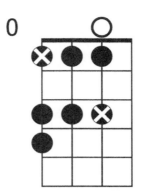
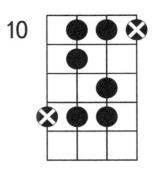

FIG.251 - DORIAN BEGINNING ON 4TH STRING

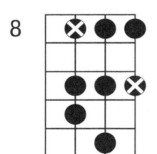
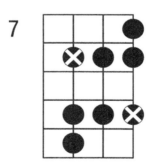
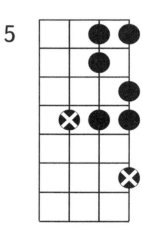

FIG.252 - DORIAN BEGINNING ON 3RD STRING

1 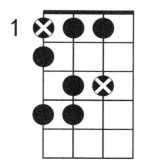   11 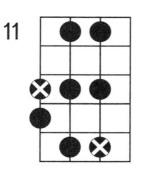   10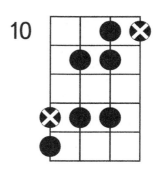

FIG.253 - PHRYGIAN BEGINNING ON 4TH STRING

8 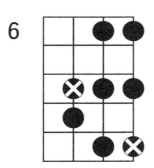   6   5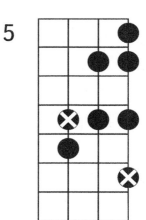

FIG.254 - PHRYGIAN BEGINNING ON 3RD STRING

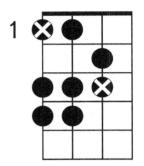

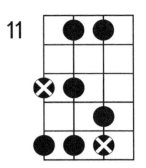

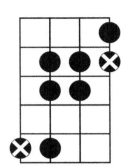

FIG.255 - HARMONIC BEGINNING ON 4TH STRING

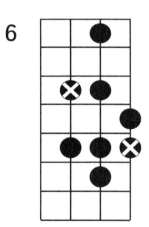

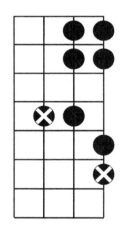

FIG.256 - HARMONIC BEGINNING ON 3RD STRING

Note: For Descending Melodic Minor, see Aeolian

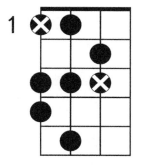
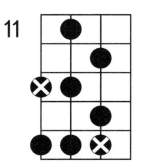
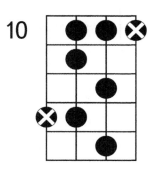

FIG.257 - MELODIC MINOR ASCENDING BEGINNING ON 4TH STRING

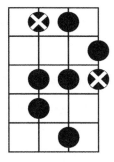
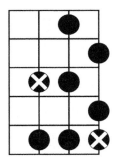
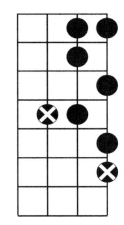

FIG.258 - MELODIC MINOR ASCENDING BEGINNING ON 3RD STRING

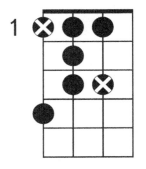

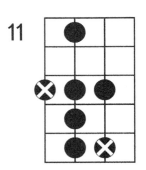

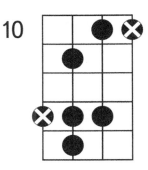

FIG.259 - BLUES SCALE BEGINNING ON 4TH STRING

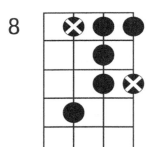

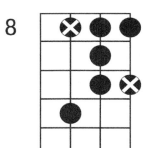

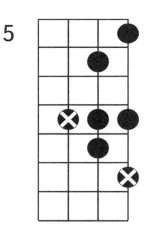

FIG.260 - BLUES SCALE BEGINNING ON 3RD STRING

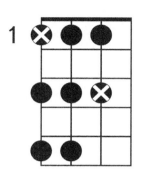
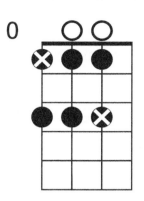
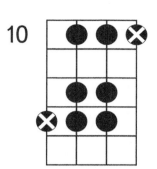

FIG.261 - MIXOLYDIAN BEGINNING ON 4TH STRING

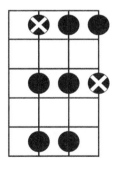
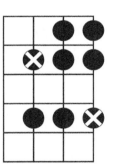
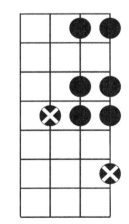

FIG.262 - MIXOLYDIAN BEGINNING ON 3RD STRING

AUGMENTED TYPES

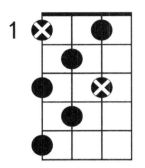
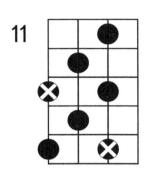
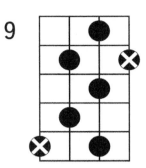

FIG.263 - WHOLE TONE BEGINNING ON 4TH STRING

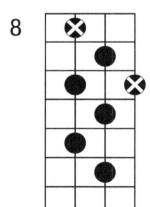
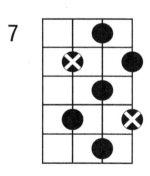
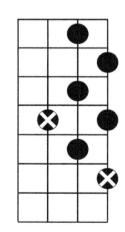

FIG.264 - WHOLE TONE BEGINNING ON 3RD STRING

DIMINISHED TYPES

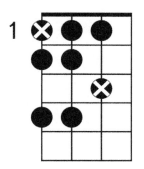
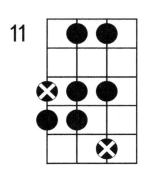
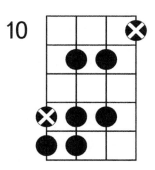

FIG.265 - LOCRIAN BEGINNING ON 4TH STRING

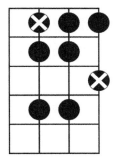
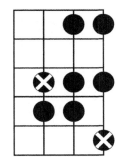

FIG.266 - LOCRIAN BEGINNING ON 3RD STRING

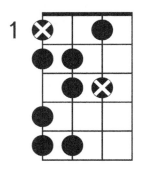 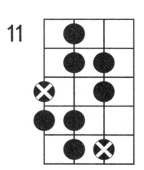 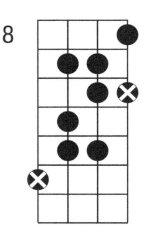

FIG.267 - HALF/WHOLE DIMINISHED BEGINNING ON 4TH STRING

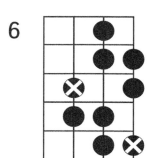

FIG.268 - HALF/WHOLE DIMINISHED BEGINNING ON 3RD STRING

SCALES WITH ROOT = F SHARP/G FLAT

MAJOR TYPES

IONIAN (MAJOR)

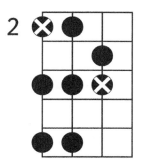

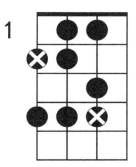

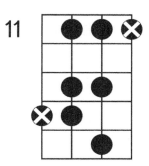

FIG.269 - IONIAN BEGINNING ON 4TH STRING

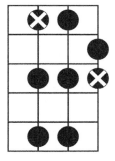

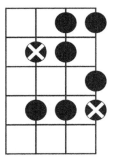

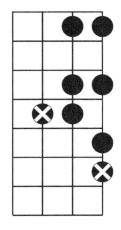

FIG.270 - IONIAN BEGINNING ON 3RD STRING

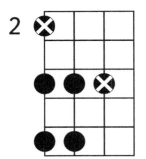
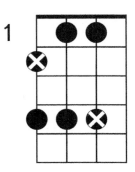
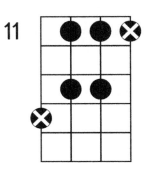

FIG.271 - MAJOR PENTATONIC BEGINNING ON 4TH STRING

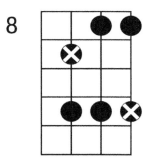
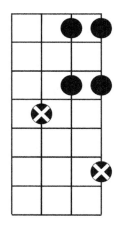

FIG.272 - MAJOR PENTATONIC BEGINNING ON 3RD STRING

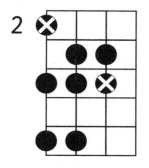
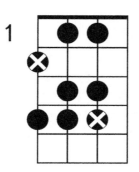
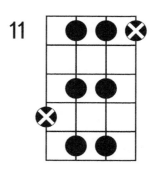

FIG.273 - LYDIAN BEGINNING ON 4TH STRING

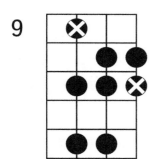
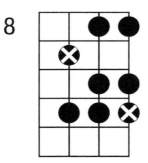
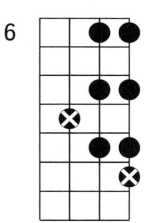

FIG.274 - LYDIAN BEGINNING ON 3RD STRING

AEOLIAN (NATURAL MINOR)

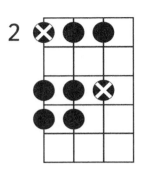
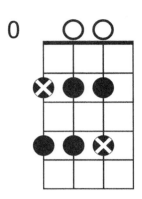
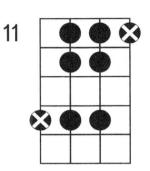

FIG.275 - AEOLIAN BEGINNING ON 4TH STRING

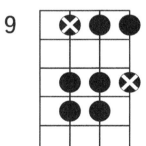
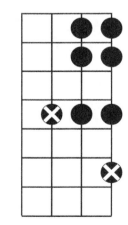

FIG.276 - AEOLIAN BEGINNING ON 3RD STRING

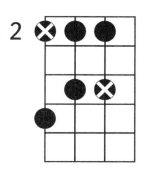
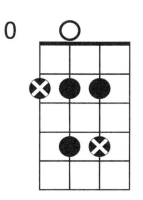
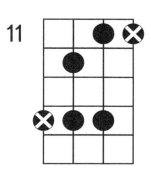

FIG.277 - MINOR PENTATONIC BEGINNING ON 4TH STRING

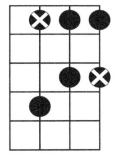
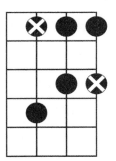
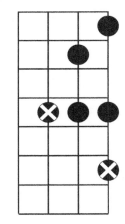

FIG.278 - MINOR PENTATONIC BEGINNING ON 3RD STRING

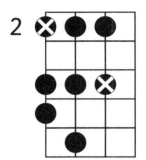
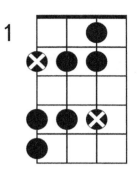
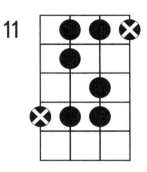

FIG.279 - DORIAN BEGINNING ON 4TH STRING

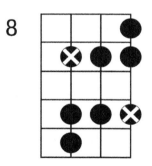
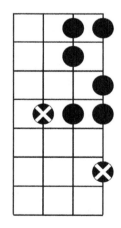

FIG.280 - DORIAN BEGINNING ON 3RD STRING

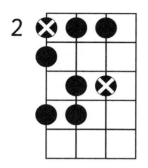
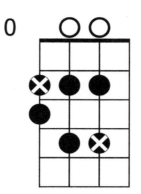
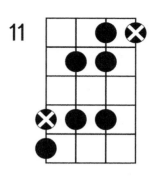

FIG.281 - PHRYGIAN BEGINNING ON 4TH STRING

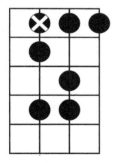
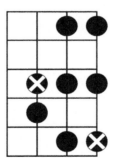
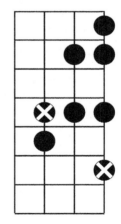

FIG.282 - PHRYGIAN BEGINNING ON 3RD STRING

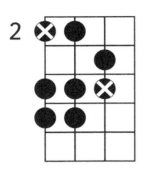
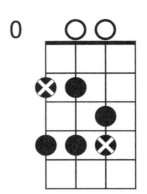
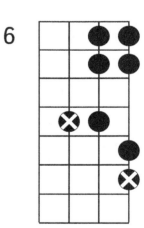

FIG.283 - HARMONIC BEGINNING ON 4TH STRING

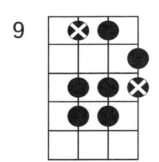
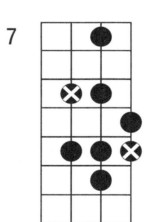

FIG.284 - HARMONIC BEGINNING ON 3RD STRING

Note: For Descending Melodic Minor, see Aeolian

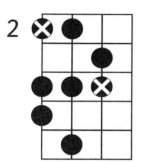
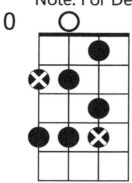
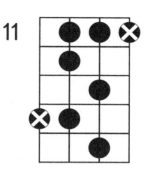

FIG.285 - MELODIC MINOR ASCENDING BEGINNING ON 4TH STRING

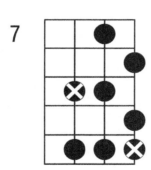
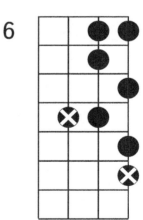

FIG.286 - MELODIC MINOR ASCENDING BEGINNING ON 3RD STRING

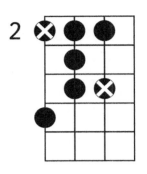
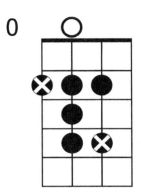
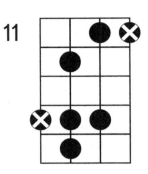

FIG.287 - BLUES SCALE BEGINNING ON 4TH STRING

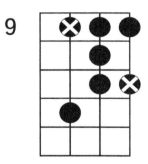
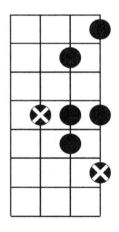

FIG.288 - BLUES SCALE BEGINNING ON 3RD STRING

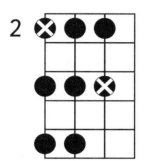
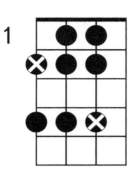
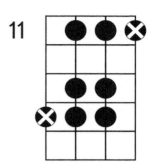

FIG.289 - MIXOLYDIAN BEGINNING ON 4TH STRING

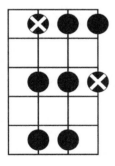
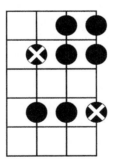
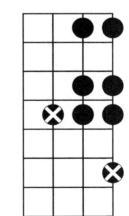

FIG.290 - MIXOLYDIAN BEGINNING ON 3RD STRING

AUGMENTED TYPES

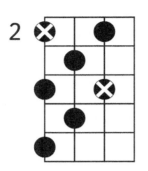
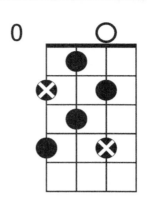
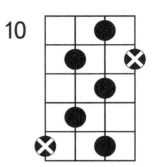

FIG.291 - WHOLE TONE BEGINNING ON 4TH STRING

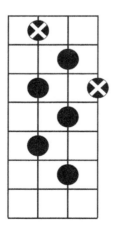
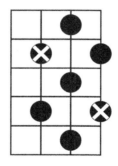
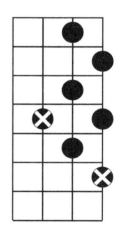

FIG.292 - WHOLE TONE BEGINNING ON 3RD STRING

DIMINISHED TYPES

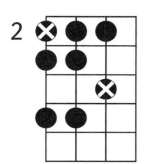

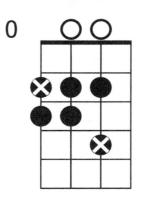

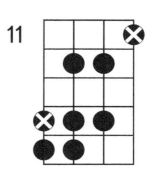

FIG.293 - LOCRIAN BEGINNING ON 4TH STRING

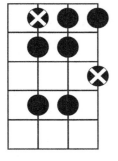

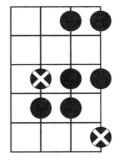

FIG.294 - LOCRIAN BEGINNING ON 3RD STRING

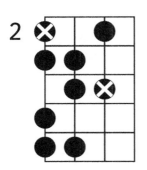
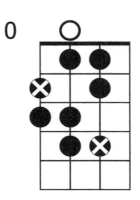
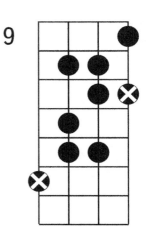

FIG.295 - HALF/WHOLE DIMINISHED BEGINNING ON 4TH STRING

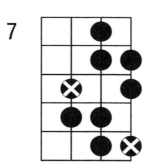

FIG.296 - HALF/WHOLE DIMINISHED BEGINNING ON 3RD STRING

SCALES WITH ROOT = G

MAJOR TYPES

IONIAN (MAJOR)

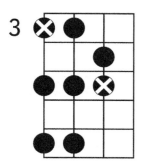
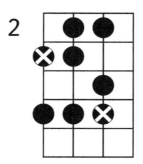
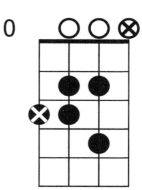

FIG.297 - IONIAN BEGINNING ON 4TH STRING

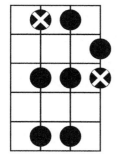
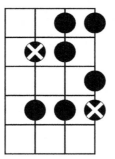
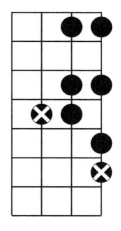

FIG.298 - IONIAN BEGINNING ON 3RD STRING

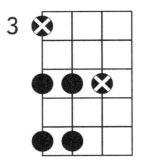
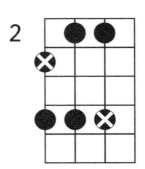
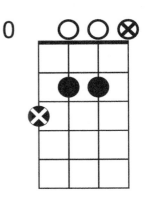

FIG.299 - MAJOR PENTATONIC BEGINNING ON 4TH STRING

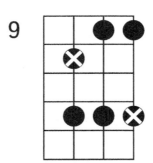
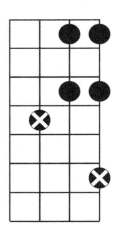

FIG.300 - MAJOR PENTATONIC BEGINNING ON 3RD STRING

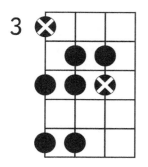
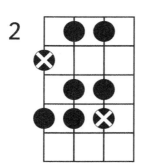
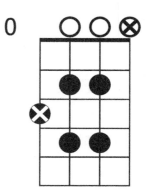

FIG.301 - LYDIAN BEGINNING ON 4TH STRING

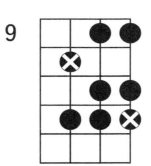
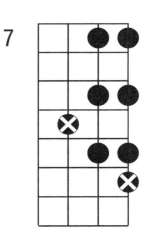

FIG.302 - LYDIAN BEGINNING ON 3RD STRING

MINOR TYPES
AEOLIAN (NATURAL MINOR)

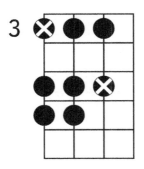
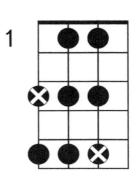
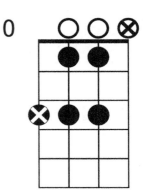

FIG.303 - AEOLIAN BEGINNING ON 4TH STRING

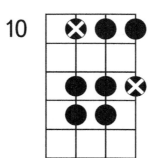
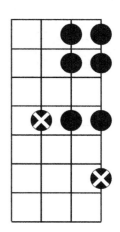

FIG.304 - AEOLIAN BEGINNING ON 3RD STRING

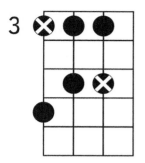
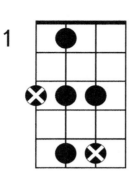
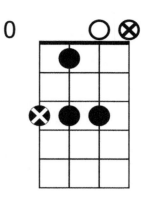

FIG.305 - MINOR PENTATONIC BEGINNING ON 4TH STRING

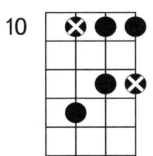
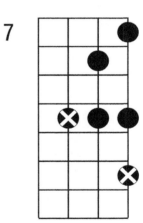

FIG.306 - MINOR PENTATONIC BEGINNING ON 3RD STRING

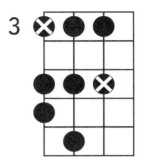

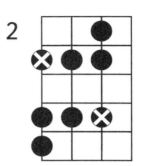

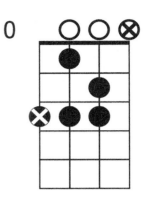

FIG.307 - DORIAN BEGINNING ON 4TH STRING

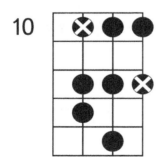

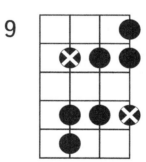

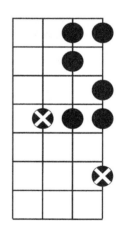

FIG.308 - DORIAN BEGINNING ON 3RD STRING

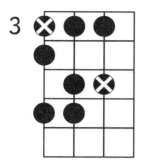
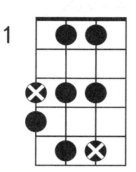
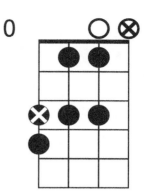

FIG.309 - PHRYGIAN BEGINNING ON 4TH STRING

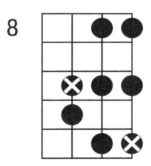
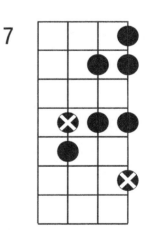

FIG.310 - PHRYGIAN BEGINNING ON 3RD STRING

3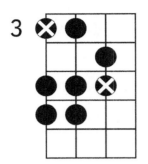

1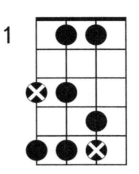

11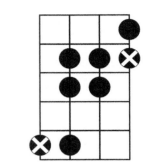

FIG.311 - HARMONIC BEGINNING ON 4TH STRING

10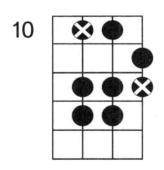

8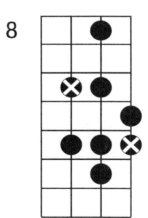

7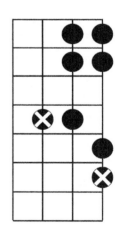

FIG.312 - HARMONIC BEGINNING ON 3RD STRING

Note: For Descending Melodic Minor, see Aeolian

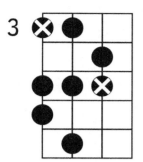 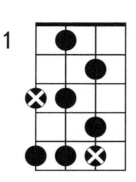 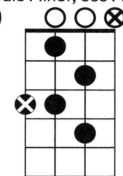

FIG.313 - MELODIC MINOR ASCENDING BEGINNING ON 4TH STRING

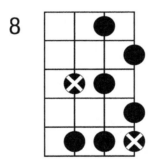 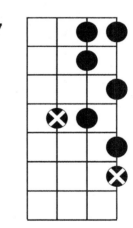

FIG.314 - MELODIC MINOR ASCENDING BEGINNING ON 3RD STRING

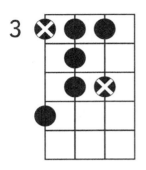
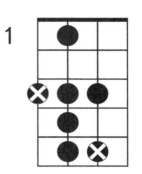
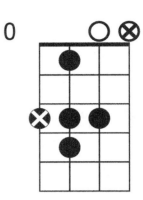

FIG.315 - BLUES SCALE BEGINNING ON 4TH STRING

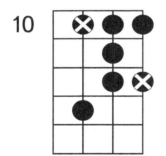
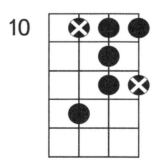
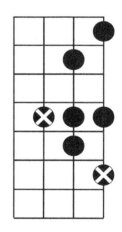

FIG.316 - BLUES SCALE BEGINNING ON 3RD STRING

DOMINANT TYPES

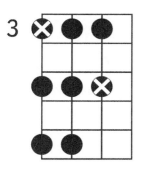 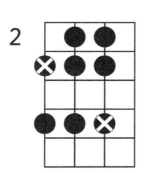 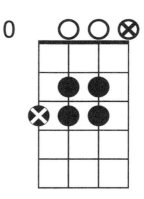

FIG.317 - MIXOLYDIAN BEGINNING ON 4TH STRING

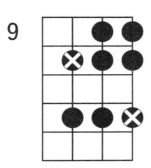 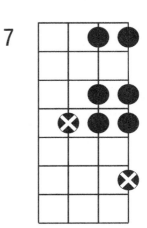

FIG.318 - MIXOLYDIAN BEGINNING ON 3RD STRING

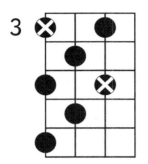 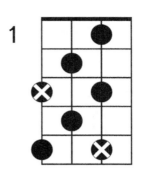 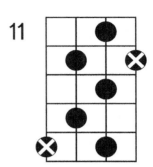

FIG.319 - WHOLE TONE BEGINNING ON 4TH STRING

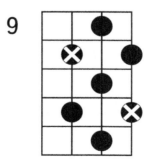 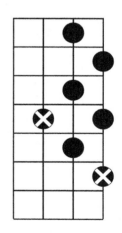

FIG.320 - WHOLE TONE BEGINNING ON 3RD STRING

DIMINISHED TYPES

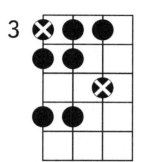
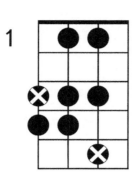
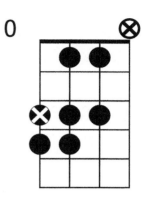

FIG.321 - LOCRIAN BEGINNING ON 4TH STRING

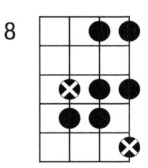

FIG.322 - LOCRIAN BEGINNING ON 3RD STRING

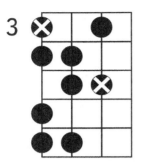
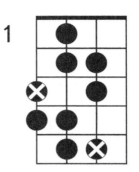
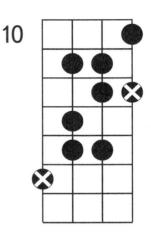

FIG.323 - HALF/WHOLE DIMINISHED BEGINNING ON 4TH STRING

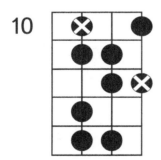
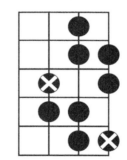

FIG.324 - HALF/WHOLE DIMINISHED BEGINNING ON 3RD STRING

SCALES WITH ROOT = G SHARP/A FLAT

MAJOR TYPES

IONIAN (MAJOR)

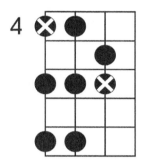

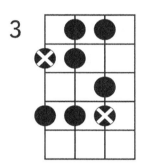

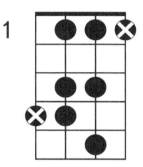

FIG.325 - IONIAN BEGINNING ON 4TH STRING

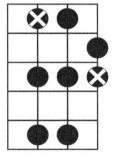

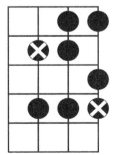

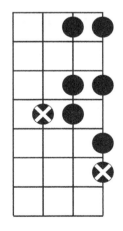

FIG.326 - IONIAN BEGINNING ON 3RD STRING

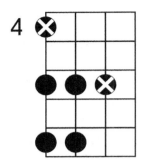

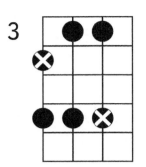

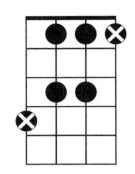

FIG.327 - MAJOR PENTATONIC BEGINNING ON 4TH STRING

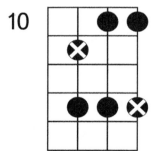

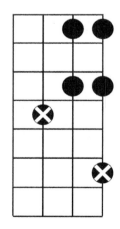

FIG.328 - MAJOR PENTATONIC BEGINNING ON 3RD STRING

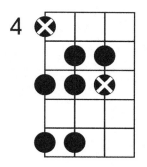

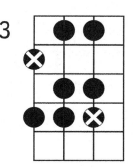

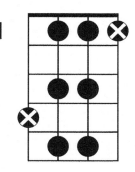

FIG.329 - LYDIAN BEGINNING ON 4TH STRING

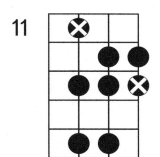

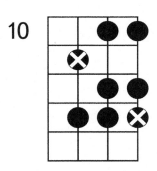

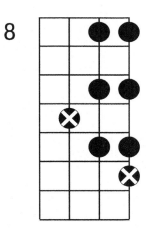

FIG.330 - LYDIAN BEGINNING ON 3RD STRING

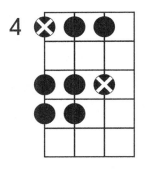
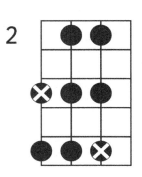
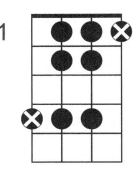

FIG.331 - AEOLIAN BEGINNING ON 4TH STRING

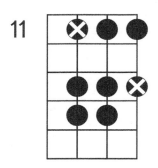
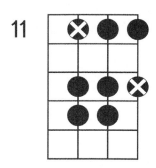
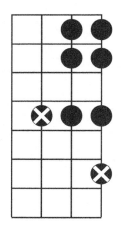

FIG.332 - AEOLIAN BEGINNING ON 3RD STRING

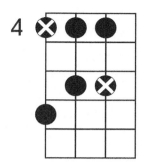 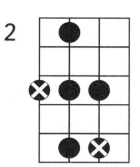 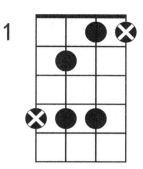

FIG.333 - MINOR PENTATONIC BEGINNING ON 4TH STRING

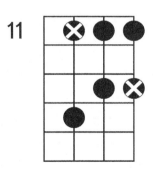 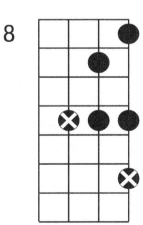

FIG.334 - MINOR PENTATONIC BEGINNING ON 3RD STRING

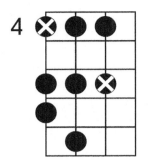

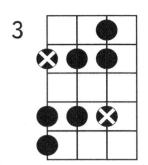

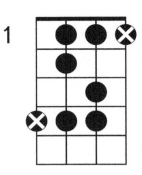

FIG.335 - DORIAN BEGINNING ON 4TH STRING

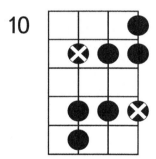

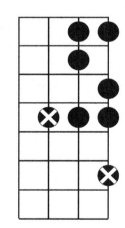

FIG.336 - DORIAN BEGINNING ON 3RD STRING

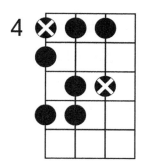 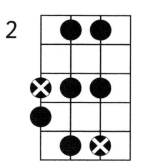 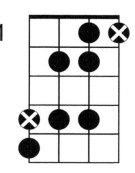

FIG.337 - PHRYGIAN BEGINNING ON 4TH STRING

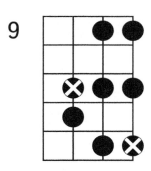 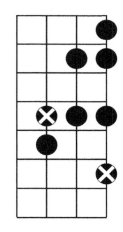

FIG.338 - PHRYGIAN BEGINNING ON 3RD STRING

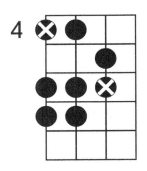 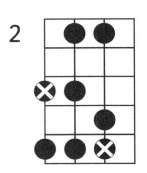 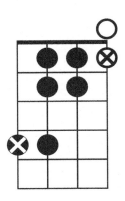

FIG.339 - HARMONIC BEGINNING ON 4TH STRING

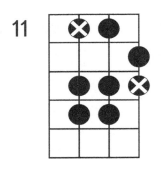 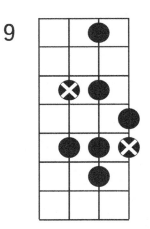 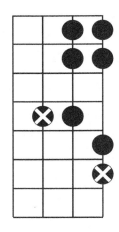

FIG.340 - HARMONIC BEGINNING ON 3RD STRING

Note: For Descending Melodic Minor, see Aeolian

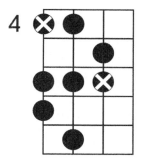
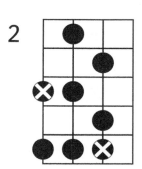
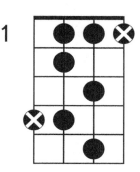

FIG.341 - MELODIC MINOR ASCENDING BEGINNING ON 4TH STRING

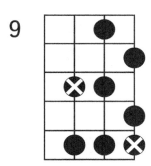
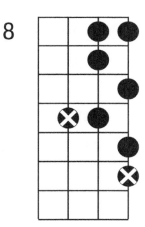

FIG.342 - MELODIC MINOR ASCENDING BEGINNING ON 3RD STRING

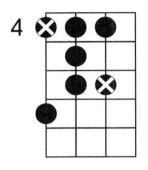 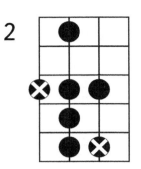 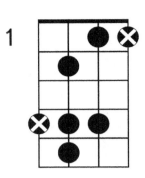

FIG.343 - BLUES SCALE BEGINNING ON 4TH STRING

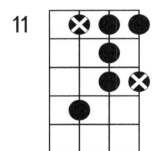 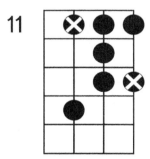 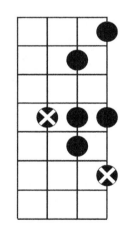

FIG.344 - BLUES SCALE BEGINNING ON 3RD STRING

DOMINANT TYPES

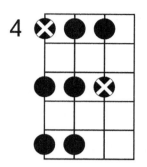

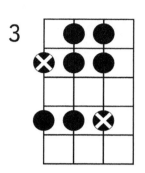

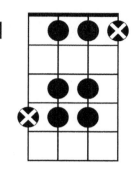

FIG.345 - MIXOLYDIAN BEGINNING ON 4TH STRING

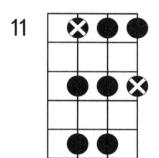

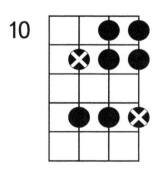

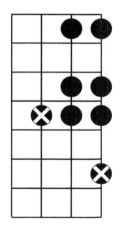

FIG.346 - MIXOLYDIAN BEGINNING ON 3RD STRING

AUGMENTED TYPES

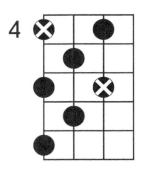
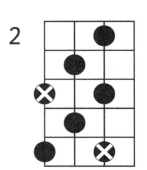
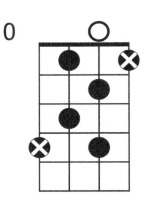

FIG.347 - WHOLE TONE BEGINNING ON 4TH STRING

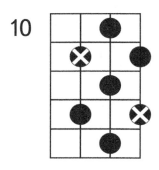
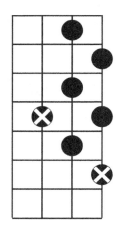

FIG.348 - WHOLE TONE BEGINNING ON 3RD STRING

DIMINISHED TYPES

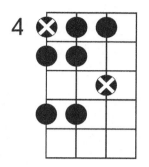 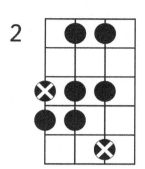 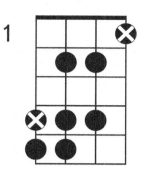

FIG.349 - LOCRIAN BEGINNING ON 4TH STRING

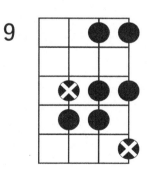

FIG.350 - LOCRIAN BEGINNING ON 3RD STRING

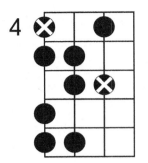
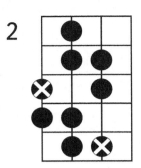
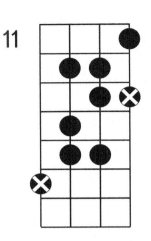

FIG.351 - Half/Whole Diminished Beginning on 4th String

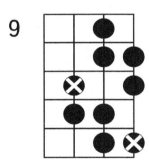

FIG.352 - Half/Whole Diminished Beginning on 3rd String

CHROMATIC SCALES

These chromatic scales are presented without a given key. Dots with X's indicate the root.

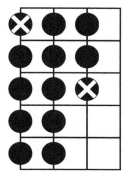 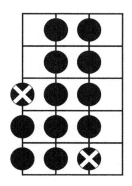 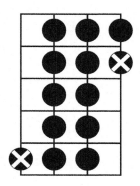

FIG.353 - CHROMATIC BEGINNING ON 4TH STRING

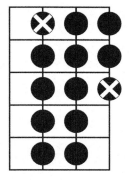 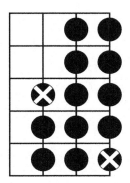 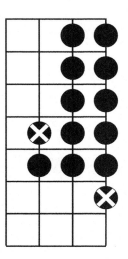

FIG.354 - CHROMATIC BEGINNING ON 3RD STRING

Printed in Great Britain
by Amazon